Waiting For Lucinda

One Family's International Adoption Journey

Amy Shore

PublishAmerica
Baltimore

First printing

ISBN: 1-4137-4383-8

PUBLISHED BY PUBLISHAMERICA, LLLP

www.publishamerica.com

Baltimore

Printed in the United States of America

*This book is dedicated with love to
Dave, Miranda, and Lucy.*

The author wishes to acknowledge the following:

My parents Deeny and Howard Shore for their unconditional support every single step of the way—you helped me see, even in the dark.

My beloved grandparents Lillian and Leo Shore for always believing in me.

My in-laws Alice and Larry Jean for their spontaneous enthusiasm and love for granddaughter number two.

My friends and relatives (especially Stacy, Celeste, Francis, Cousin Deb, and Aunts Jackie and Julie) whose hearts and prayers journeyed with us throughout the adoption process.

Aunt Maureen, cousin Stephen, and my grandparents Lillian and Harry Nemeth—you will always be remembered and loved.

Allan Dean, publisher of the *Atlantic Highlands Herald*, for giving me the opportunity to write an adoption column for his newspaper.

Lucinda's birthmother Odelia Rubi somewhere in Guatemala who twice gave Lucy the gift of life—I can never thank you enough.

Consuela in Guatemala City who showered Lucy with love and affection during her first year of life—you will always have a special place in my heart.

Manfred and his associates at Adoption Supervisors in Guatemala City who were as tenacious as I– you made my dream come true.

Prologue

How *Edgar Allan* Changed My Life

Back in the 1970s I read the book *Edgar Allan* by author John Neufeld. I was (and remain) a voracious reader; when I was a kid, I read books about everything and anything. But John Neufeld's book made a deep impression on me, one that would change my life twenty years later.

Edgar Allan is a story about a white pastor and his family in California who adopt an African-American boy named Edgar Allan and the impact the adoption has on their lives. Back then, the racial divide was much greater than it is today; it wasn't very common to encounter a blended family. In the book, the characters encounter prejudice and their lives get very complicated as a result of their decision to adopt, but, at the same time, they pull together and discover that love far outweighs anything else. Family is what matters. The generosity and deep caring and commitment I witnessed between these pages had a lasting impression on me. When I closed the book, I told my mother, "When I get older, I am going to adopt a child!" She was busy making dinner in the kitchen, and I remember seeing her smile.

Fast forward to 1992…

My husband Dave and I are the proud parents of a baby girl we name Miranda. For the next ten years, she is the light of our lives, the center of our attention, the air we breathe. When I became a mother, life seemed to begin, even though I did have a life before labor and delivery. Parenthood is an awesome responsibility: it is fun, exciting, and scary– a roller coaster ride I wouldn't have missed for anything in this world.

Fast forward now to 2002...

Dave and I are toying with the idea of having another child. We always wanted to have more than one, but life seemed to get in the way of those plans. We raised our daughter and climbed career ladders. For five years I was a devoted English teacher who enjoyed everything about the classroom. I loved my students as if they were my very own.

I interrupted my career in order to be home full time with Miranda. I didn't like the idea of day care, even though I do not judge those who use it. I wanted to be a hands-on mother, especially during all those important "firsts." When my daughter was ready for preschool, I returned to the classroom.

When I resumed my teaching responsibilities, I knew it would be very hard to interrupt my career again in order to have another child. But my husband and I vowed not to have another child just for the heck of having another. We wanted to have another if and when we felt the same longing and desire we had when we brought Miranda into the world.

That yearning came last summer...

The biological clock ticking, Miranda growing older and more independent, I had that strong desire to become a mother again. My husband and I talked and talked and talked about it. How would this affect my career? Now, with thirteen teaching years behind me, not only was I a teacher, but I was also a guidance counselor responsible for helping students get into college. My hours were 8 a.m. until 5 p.m. Could we handle two children and work full time without relatives in the area for support? Dave often traveled for work. Could I handle things on my own?

The biggest question: what about day care? I knew that if I interrupted my teaching now, it would be very difficult to return to it in a few years. It was hard enough to break back into my profession when I took time off for my first child. And at this point I had a supervisory position in a school that I loved. I couldn't walk away...

I made a deal with the Devil and said, "Yes," to all the questions. I knew deep in my heart that I would regret not having another child, and the thought of adding to our already close-knit family was intoxicating. So life would be hectic and chaotic! We can handle it, I thought.

After making the decision to have a baby, I was pregnant with Miranda in one month. Dave and I were 10 years younger then. This time we tried for several months with no success.

Over a soul-searching dinner one July evening in 2002, Dave simply said,

"Why don't we adopt?" Light bulbs in my brain started flashing; fireworks appeared before my eyes. I then remembered *Edgar Allan* and *immediately* embraced the idea!

It didn't matter to us if our child was biologically conceived; what mattered most was that we would become parents to a child we would love and cherish for the rest of our lives. And we loved the idea of bringing into our family a child in need of a loving forever family.

That's when we began our adoption journey…

Chapter 1:

Jumping Through Hoops To Be Parents
July, 2002

Wouldn't the world be a wonderful place if, after seeing a *Save The Children* commercial on TV, you could pick up the phone, say that you want to adopt one of those precious children, and then just fly out there and bring the little one home. And if Hollywood was a true reflection of reality, you could just go to an orphanage, fall in love at first sight with a little orphan named, say, Annie or Oliver, and bring the little one home to love and cherish forever and ever.

Well, it doesn't work that way. If you want to adopt a child, be prepared for a long wait and mounds of paperwork. It's easy to be parents if you have good eggs and sperm that work well. Heck, you don't have to be financially fit or of legal age or even answer any questions! But if you want to give an orphaned, neglected, abused, or abandoned child a home, you have to answer many, many, many questions and pass tests in order to be "deemed" acceptable parental material.

The first step is a home study. Dave, Miranda, and I had to meet with an approved, licensed New Jersey social worker four times. She had to visit our home once to make sure we didn't live in a roach-infested shack without plumbing, and then we had to give her paperwork in order for her to write a report that would say we would be good adoptive parents.

Here's the list of required documents for the home study:

• Official doctor's letters saying each of us is healthy and able to parent a child

• Official local police letters saying we were fingerprinted and we have

no criminal records
- • Fingerprint cards of our fingerprints for the FBI to process
- • Two letters of recommendation from people who know us well and can say, "Yes, they'd be good adoptive parents!"
- • One letter from a neighbor who can say we are pleasant to live near and, no, she has never seen or heard us beat children or animals.
- • A long questionnaire detailing financial, legal, moral, personal, professional, and medical information.

Both my husband and I had to write separate "autobiographies" explaining who we are, why we are who we are, why we think our parents were the way they were, what we learned from their style of parenting, who we would like to be, why we are looking to adopt a child, what type of parents we think we would be, what type of child we dream of, what type of discipline we embrace, and why we think we would be good parents.

We started the home study in July, but we didn't have the completed copy in hand until October mainly because the FBI has to process the fingerprints, and the results don't come for weeks and weeks. We had to be fingerprinted electronically by the Immigration and Naturalization Service in Newark for the FBI as well. Wouldn't you think one fingerprinting analysis would be enough? Well, no, because each set gets checked independently since no department wants to take the time to communicate back and forth. And to think that when I watch *Forensic Files* on TV, a detective only needs one darn fingerprint to make a match! Right now my fingerprints are all over the place! But I didn't commit a crime, so it takes a year and a day for the government to clear me…and because I'm not a terrorist or a murderer, there's no hurry. After all, I just want to adopt a child.

Did I mention that almost everything has a fee? Without charge the local police did our fingerprints and checked the database to make sure we were lawful citizens. That was our only "freebie."

It is important to note that if you decide to adopt a child in the state of New Jersey, you can have your home study report done without fee if you agree to be foster parents through a foster-adopt program. After you go through training to be foster parents of New Jersey children who need a safe place to live because they have been either neglected, abused, and/or their parents are unable to care for them, you may have the opportunity to adopt them—that is, if the parental rights are terminated. There are no guarantees, of course, but many, many children have found loving homes this way. It is the most economic of all adoption options.

We decided to go the private route and adopt a baby girl from Guatemala. Why Guatemala? Simple. When we told Miranda that we were considering adopting a child and asked her what she thought, she pondered this notion for a while, and then gave us her blessing. You see, her very good friend was adopted ten years ago from Guatemala, so naturally, she thought, that is the country from which we should adopt. In her mind, there was nowhere else even to consider! If she was going to share her parents and her home forever and ever, she said, it had to be with a sister. So we did our research online, by phone, through the Better Business Bureau, through word of mouth, through television documentaries, through other adoptive parents, and by reading several books about adoption, and we decided that we were a perfect match for Guatemala, a country that only requires the adoptive family to visit the country for approximately three days, and a country in which the children, most born into poverty, come home approximately four to seven months after referral. That would mean that we would have our baby girl home before she was one!

Of course, the adoption agency and the government of Guatemala require even *more* paperwork than the social worker! We had to supply more medical letters, more letters of recommendation, financial statements, INS clearance, employment verification letters, passport documentation, name affidavits, even pictures of our home and family! And every single document had to be notarized, then sent to the state department for certification that the notary is an approved notary in the state of New Jersey, and, after all that, each paper had to be sent to the Guatemalan Embassy in New York City to be officially "stamped." (The lady at the UPS Store greets me with a big smile; we are now on a first name basis. The same is true for the UPS man who delivers in my neighborhood...)

All of these papers are collected and called a "dossier." The dossier is sent to the adoption agency that sends it to a lawyer in Guatemala where every piece of paper is translated from English into Spanish. When that is done, THEN and only then is a family ready to be matched with a baby.

If you want to adopt, you really have to WANT to adopt. Maybe that's why there are so many hoops through which to jump. Almost anyone can be a biological parent, but only squeaky-clean, law-abiding, financially stable, morally centered, incredibly patient people with a high threshold for frustration and a good sense of humor can be adoptive parents.

Chapter 2:

Spreading The News
August, 2002

So how do you tell your family that you are going to adopt? This is the big question that many adopting families ponder. Ours was no exception. After we had our daughter Miranda, our relatives were waiting to hear more baby announcements, but after four or five years, that seemed to fade. Of course, we did get the "so when are you going to give Miranda a brother or sister?" comments, hints that we were being monitored. But when nothing materialized, people got the hint and left us alone to live our lives the way we wanted to live them. We were very happy raising an only child, and our only was very happy being the only child.

When Miranda turned 10, we three decided that we were going to do some adventurous international travel. Miranda made a list of countries for us to see together: England, Israel, France, Ireland, Italy, Australia....With only one child, there is more money to do such exploring. What an educational opportunity, we thought! Our two salaries would definitely make this a reality. But what we didn't expect, and what no one could even imagine, was September 11th in 2001.

Like so many Americans, our lives changed after that incredibly tragic day. What we used to take for granted we examined more closely. The world was not the same. Neither were our priorities.

After witnessing on TV, rerun after rerun after rerun, of those airplanes crashing into the Twin Towers, Miranda and I were too afraid to fly. So the international travel was postponed. I started to think about what is really important in life. What is it that we *really* cling to and cherish above all else?

Like other Americans shocked that we were victims of terrorism, I began to think about what I would miss the most if I were not to see tomorrow. And my eyes filled with tears when I thought about never seeing my beautiful daughter and wonderful husband ever again. Family was what was most important. So, very simply, our focus shifted from career and travel to what was in our hearts. And for the first time in a very long time, we wanted to have a baby.

If we had a baby, we wouldn't be able to take those extravagant vacations we planned. But then again, we didn't want to fly during terror alerts. If we had a baby, the purse strings would have to be pulled tighter. But then again, we had enough money for the necessities and even some luxuries. After all, this is what we worked for...for our family. If we had a baby, we'd be happy. If we had a baby, we'd be adding more love and joy into our lives. If we had a baby, our daughter would know the love of a sibling. The positives outweighed the negatives...

Then we decided to adopt. Then we decided to tell the relatives.

My parents, retired and living in Florida, were speechless. "Why?" was all they could utter at first. This decision totally surprised them. "You have a beautiful daughter, a wonderful career, a good marriage...Why? Your life is set!"

I never thought my life at the age of 37 was etched in stone. Set. Never to change. I explained to them on the phone *why* we wanted to adopt, *how* we were going to adopt, *where* we were going to adopt, *who* we were going to adopt. "It's a blessing, what you're doing," said my father, when it all sunk in; then he asked if we were planning to adopt a Jewish Guatemalan baby. Some things, especially in a Jewish family, never change! My parents, once they were informed and did their own research on foreign adoption, embraced the idea. They were excited! Another grandchild!

My in-laws, retired and living in New Hampshire, were ecstatic! They knew someone who recently adopted children from China. They thought it was terrific that we were going to adopt a baby. Another grandchild!

Our siblings were happy, too. But how to tell my grandparents?

My Massachusetts paternal grandmother, Nana, 84, and my paternal grandfather, Zadie, 88, smiled, their eyes danced, when we told them we were adopting a baby. (Whatever I do they think is grand...) Sometimes they amaze me with their open-mindedness.

Lastly, we flew to Florida and told my 87-year old maternal grandfather Poppy and other relatives the news.

"You're adopting *what*?" he asked.

"A baby!" I answered, enthusiastically. My great Aunt Jackie and Uncle Irving were overjoyed! My mother's sister Julie and her husband George beamed! So did my Mom and Dad. But my grandfather and his lady friend were somewhat confused.

"For how long?" asked my grandfather, rather perplexed. No one in the family had ever adopted.

"Forever, Poppy," I said, smiling. *Forever.*

Then I explained all the details. Dave and I answered many questions. I told my grandfather we were naming our baby after my grandmother, his wife Lillian, my Nanny, who died five years earlier. He was deeply touched.

"I'm proud of you, Amy," said my grandfather as we were preparing to leave. I smiled and kissed him goodbye.

And that was the last time I saw him. He suddenly died three weeks later.

Life changes. Just when you think you have a handle on things, they alter without your permission. That's when you realize that you really *don't* have control over anything, but you *do* have the ability to make decisions and affect change in your life. Family is very important to me. That love is something fixed in an ever-changing world. And what better way to affect eternity and family than to add more love to the mix? *With* us, *our families* were adopting a baby too...

Chapter 3:

God Works In Mysterious Ways...
September, 2002

I am a very spiritual person. I really do believe that God works in mysterious ways. And when something big happens in my life, I think it's divinely inspired. Sure, I can make poor decisions, but I really think that there is a reason for everything, and sometimes through those "mistakes" I learn and grow; sometimes by taking risks and making changes, I continue down the path that God intended for me all along.

This has been a big year in my life for divine intervention. First, Dave and I decided to have another baby. We tried to conceive a child for several months, and the results were not to be desired. We started the paper-chasing phase of the adoption process. Then my maternal grandfather suddenly died. I was "ripe" for frustration, disappointment, and sadness.

I remember watching Poppy's coffin being lowered into the ground, thinking, *this is the end of something major in my life*. My mother's parents were no longer alive; I was moving up the line in the family; I was thinking about me at the age of 87 and what I would be able to look back on. Would I have regrets?

I gazed through tears at the stone marking my beloved grandparents' final resting place. All those theater shows they introduced me to when I was young, the trips into Brooklyn by train to see my great grandmother, the week long visits to their Connecticut home that I took by bus by myself in the summertime, the moment we witnessed together on TV President Nixon's resignation ("This is history in the making," said Poppy, solemn, his face white, staring at the screen.) The unending words of Jewish and secular wisdom I learned from my Nanny that I continue to live by. "This too shall pass," she would often say to me when something went wrong, her face wrinkled in a perpetual smile. Her convictions made me believe she was right.

And this is what I whispered to myself as I left the cemetery that morning. Nanny was right again. This grief will pass…and so will this empty feeling…

But they lingered into a clinical depression.

And in that intense grief that I felt, I believe God opened my eyes and made me see my life in a way I had never seen it before. Thoughts flooded my mind. Memories flashed before my eyes. My responsibilities as a wife, mother, daughter, friend, and teacher weighed heavily on me, yet I could not focus nor concentrate. My stomach didn't want to digest, and every night I restlessly tossed and turned under the covers. I was not functioning well. I was sick.

I had a lot of thinking time. Some realizations hit me like a ton of bricks:

My daughter Miranda was moving into the tween and adolescent years, and I wanted to be there for her full-time, hands on, without distractions. I knew this is when she would need me the most. Being a high school teacher for many years was a great insight into the needs of adolescents. Over the past thirteen years I was there for so many of my students when they really needed me, but how could I *not* be there for my own when she hit those difficult, exciting, challenging years of her life?

The Adoption and Day Care "deal" that I made with the Devil came back to haunt me. My baby would be coming from a third-world nation to America to live with and be loved by her forever family, and it physically hurt my heart to think about putting her into day care from 7 a.m. until 6 p.m. in order to keep my foot in the career door. But that's what I decided I would do when we decided to add to our family. I knew that our baby *deserved* more than that. I wanted to be her *mother*, and that schedule would keep her an *orphan*.

After many years of constantly being on the go, I was physically and emotionally exhausted. It was time to think about what was best for me. Never before did I ever put my needs first. It was time for me to break those cement blocks of stress that were weighing me down after years of balancing everything on just my two shoulders. If I didn't, I wouldn't be able to keep my head above water; I'd drown. It was time to realize I was only one person and there was no cape with a big "S" on my back.

The last day I saw Poppy in Florida, he asked me something that stuck with me long after the plane ride home. "How is this adoption going to affect *you*?" he said. I wasn't able to answer him then. I shrugged my shoulders. I was just happy and knew it would all work out. I knew how adopting a baby would affect my family, my house, my wallet, my teaching…but I didn't look deep into the crevices of my soul to know how it would deeply affect *me*. And that's when God knocked me down with those months of self-reflection.

After writing important college recommendations for my high school students, I resigned the job I loved. It was time for me to reclaim what was most important to me. I had been coming and going between the walls of my house, but it was really just a bus stop of sorts. I left in the morning and I returned in the evening, going to sleep and waking up in it, but most of the time it was just a place to house the groceries.

In the beginning I used my time to make our house a home again, a place where I knew where everything was in the cabinets and drawers, a place where I could cook dinner and not rely on take-out as often as we did in the past, a place where I felt comfortable, safe, happy and content, a place where my family and I laughed and loved and lived. (I believe the experts call this 'nesting.')

It was also time for me to "smell the flowers." I took walks in the neighborhood. I learned how to crochet. I made new friends and kept in better touch with the old. Now this former literature teacher read books for enjoyment and fulfillment rather than assignment. I got to know my eccentric cats and notice all their wonderful, unique quirks. I learned as much as possible about Guatemala and adoption. I kept in touch with former students. I reconnected with my best friend Carolyn in Rhode Island who knew me way back when in high school. I devoted time to my writing, something I always loved. I even took time to watch *Court TV*, a decadent pleasure, sometimes for several hours in the middle of a day, something foreign to a woman whose every minute in life used to be meticulously planned and highly purposeful. It was liberating!

Now my favorite time of the day is 8:20 a.m. when Miranda and I get into the car and drive to her school. We watch cartoons and eat breakfast together every morning, and those talks we have in the car are golden. In those little, stray moments, I learn so much about Miranda. We have always been close, but we're much closer now. I didn't know what I was missing. I'm glad I found out.

Now there's no more rushing. I know that if Miranda wakes up not feeling well, I don't have to juggle a million school tasks and make early morning phone calls in order to stay home and 'mother' her. Around noon every day now Dave calls me from work, and for the first time in a long time, we actually talk. I have the time to *hear* what he is saying. I talk on the phone with my mother in Florida every single morning, and I trade "instant messages" on the computer with my father every afternoon. And nightly at 5:30 p.m., my husband, daughter, and I sit at the table and eat dinner as a family.

I especially love the precious time I daydream about the daughter that I don't yet know who right now lives in my heart.

Life is good again. Sure, I miss the classroom. I miss the salary I was making. I miss the students most of all. But I love my time that I've reclaimed for me. I'm building a new life, and it's good. It's fulfilling. It's different than the lives of most women my age in today's modern world, but I have learned that each one of us has to do what is best for her, that this is our one shot at life, and we each have to leave our own unique marks on the world.

God works in mysterious ways. He was whispering, "To thine own self be true," and this year I finally heard Him.

Chapter 4:

The Call That Awakens Your Heart
November, 2002

Thursday, November 7, 2002. 3:00 p.m. This is a day and a time that has unforgettably made family history.

Miranda and I were returning home from shopping; we looked at the green blinking light on the caller ID machine and knew someone telephoned but didn't leave a message. (Technology is a wonderful thing!) Miranda investigated further and called out the telephone number. My heart started to beat faster.

"It's the adoption agency," I said to Miranda, whose eyes widened and an instant smile spread across her face.

"Mom, maybe it's about our baby!" she exclaimed, jumping up and down and prematurely celebrating.

"I bet they just have a question," I told her, "because if they had baby news, they would have left us a message to call them back."

"But, Mom, maybe there *is* news!" Miranda continued, bursting at the seams. "Let's call back!"

After checking my email and seeing no message from the agency, I picked up the telephone and dialed the office, explaining that, though I didn't have a message on the machine, I did see that they called earlier, and maybe...

"Amy, hold a minute, please," I abruptly heard on the other end of the line.

"We're on hold," I told an eager Miranda who was pacing up and down the kitchen floor just like an expectant father-to-be outside a delivery room. Soon there was another voice on the line, this time the agency's director.

"Amy? Are you sitting down?"

Oh, boy, I thought, and quickly plunked myself down in a chair. I made Miranda sit down next to me. My heart beat wildly. This was the moment we had been waiting for…

"We have a beautiful baby girl available for adoption, but we have no information on her just yet, just pictures. We are going to email them to you right now," I heard her say.

I hung up the phone, and Miranda and I raced down the stairs to the computer. Miranda was giggling and clapping her hands, elated by the news. We could not log onto the computer fast enough, my hands shaking and the password incorrectly entered twice! But, with a couple of clicks, in a matter of seconds, there she was, right before our eyes.

"Mom, there's my sister! There's my sister!" Miranda squealed, pointing at the computer and hugging me. "She's your daughter, Mom, and my sister!"

I stared at the screen. I couldn't believe my eyes. I had not envisioned what my second daughter would look like, but when I laid my eyes on her, I knew it was she, and my heart instantaneously embraced her.

There, thousands of miles away, in another country was this precious little being with dark eyes and dark hair, kissable baby cheeks, wearing a light blue dress with pink flowers and a pink bow. I counted five tiny fingers on each of her hands. She was sitting in the lap of a woman I did not know, in a place I did not recognize. I had no knowledge of her birthday, her biological family's circumstances, or her medical history.

It was love at first sight.

After printing a picture of our baby, Miranda ran up the stairs and out the door to greet her dad, just coming home from work, with the wonderful news. I called the adoption agency and stumbled over my words, trying to express the joy and elation they sent us through email. They, on the other end of the phone, laughed and shared in our happiness; they go through this several times a week, but it's still something that touches them deeply. This is their life work, bringing together families from different corners of the world, connecting little newborn lives with those adults who love them before they even enter the world.

That evening, Dave, Miranda, and I were stunned, excited, elated, full of joy, filled to the brim with happiness. Our dream was coming true; our family was becoming complete.

Somewhere out there was our baby who was unaware that her family was rejoicing her birth and daydreaming about her wonderfully bright future.

She did not yet know that awaiting her was a ten-year-old "big" sister, a mom and a dad who already cherished her, and relatives who couldn't wait to add her name to the branches of the family tree.

And so began the wait...

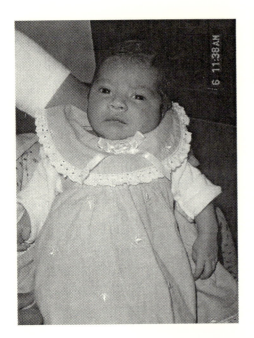 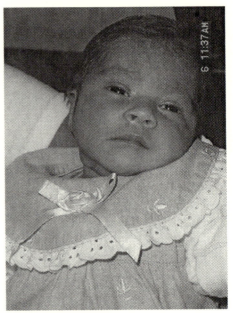

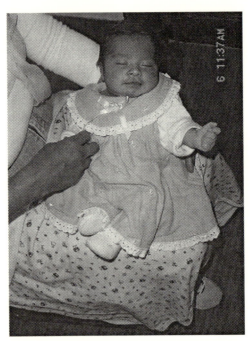

These are three of six referral photos that we received via email on November 7th from the adoption agency. No name, date of birth, or height and weight information is known at this time.

Chapter 5:

Waiting

I thought that once we were matched with a baby, I'd be so overjoyed that the adoption was actually "starting," that I'd be calmer. Not a chance! It's actually the opposite. Now that all the paperwork is done and we have baby news, I don't have anything to do but wait…and wait…and wait… And worry. What if something goes wrong? Who is caring for the baby? When will we be able to fly out and bring our baby home to New Jersey? What do we have to do to secure her a passport? What about a birth certificate? Readoption—what exactly is that?

As you can see, it is easy to torture yourself during the wait.

And did I say *all* the paperwork was done? Not a chance!

After reviewing the meager medical information (blood type, negative test results for diseases) and falling in love with our baby's picture, we had to start the ball rolling, so to speak. So up the hill we climbed back to the bank for a certified check with many zeros at the end to pay the adoption agency (who pays the lawyer in Guatemala who pays the foster mother who cares for the child) and a notary stamp on our power of attorney document so the Guatemalan lawyer can represent us through the Guatemalan court system.

Then off we dashed to the UPS store to send our adoption agency our first payment and signed adoption contract (which pretty much states that if anything goes wrong, it's not the agency's fault…).

When that envelope was sealed, another one was produced for our power of attorney (and of course the always-required check) that had to make its way first to the state department to be certified that, yes, indeed, this notary is a valid New Jersey notary (isn't that what the notary stamp is for?!) and then, in a week, when it returns to us via UPS with the envelope we provide to the state department (ca-ching!), I make my way to the UPS store again with a certified check in my hand to send this document, now notarized and state-department certified, to the Guatemalan Embassy on Park Avenue in Manhattan to be "authenticated."

Yes, another two UPS envelopes…ca-ching, ca-ching! Authenticated means that someone at the embassy rubber-stamps and signs the document that, yes, the notary stamp and the state department stamp are there as required. (Do they read the documents? Nah! Sometimes after all that, the fancy-stamped documents get 'kicked out' of the Guatemalan courts because there is a typo or something required is missing, and, oh yes, you have to start the "stamping" process all over again with a new original document until it, weeks later, gets to Guatemala again for translation from English to Spanish and then back to the court official who was reviewing the file way back when.)

After the embassy cashes our check and returns our document via UPS (our prepaid envelope!), then I return, yes, AGAIN, to the UPS store to send the power of attorney document with all the glorified stamps attached to it to the adoption agency whose director overnights it to Guatemala to their lawyer who then has it translated from English to Spanish and submits it to the courts…and we WAIT until it gets stamped and activated in Guatemala.

Foreign adoption and the word 'wait' are synonymous. Don't let anyone tell you differently.

You have to *wait* on the social worker in the United States to write a report about you and your family and the reasons why you want to adopt; you have to *wait* to gather all of your dossier documents and get the required stamps for each and every one; you have to *wait* in a long line outside the not-very-friendly INS office to get fingerprinted, you have to *wait* months to get those fingerprints processed by the United States government; you have to *wait* to get INS to approve you as adoptive parents; you have to *wait* to be matched with a baby; and then you have to *wait* to get the proper documents and fees in order that the actual adoption can begin. And then you *wait* and *wait* and *wait* for the adoption file to make its way through the courts in a foreign country whose laws are different than those we take for granted here in North America; information trickles in every now and then so you know what the delays are for…but rarely do they make sense.

I think the very first question on the home study questionnaire that is given to you on a clipboard by the United States social worker should be, *"Are you a good wait-er? Please give proof if you answer 'yes.' If you answer 'no,' put down your pencil and go home now!"*

I've figured out that I'm not such a bad wait-er after all…but please don't quote me. I may have to deny I said that to those who have heard me whine and complain and cry at times when the waiting has made me extremely frustrated and crazy. Luckily, that hasn't been daily…but weekly? Oh yes!

My world hasn't been the same since I've been "sitting on my nest," waiting…

Chapter 6:

What's In A Name?

Our baby was born in Guatemala City, named by either her birthmother or the attorney. When we first looked at her pictures, the baby had no name; information was forthcoming. So like any expectant mom, I needed to consider what name my second daughter would carry with her throughout her life. It's no easy task when you think of it that way!

Miranda loved pouring over the baby name book. In fact, ten years ago Dave and I leafed through that very same book when we were thinking about what to name *her*. So now we had another big decision to make, and there were three opinions this time to consider!

One thing was certain. Being Jewish, we were following religious naming protocol. In the Jewish tradition, a Jewish baby is named for relatives who are no longer alive. It is a way to preserve and honor their memories and accomplishments in life. It is a direct link in the chain of a Jewish family.

Ten years ago, Dave and I wanted to name our baby after my first cousin Stephen who was only twenty-five when he died. I was close to him, and I wanted the caring, gentle, loving ways he had during his short life to be passed along to my child. Steve's mother, my mother's older sister Maureen, was thrilled when I told her that our baby, boy or girl, would be named after Steve and take his Hebrew name *Shimon*. *Emily Sarah* was the girl name we chose and *Evan David* was the boy name. (If you're curious, *Emily* was in honor of the English author and poet Emily Bronte who stole my heart in high school when I read *Wuthering Heights*; *David* is my husband's first name and this would have honored his family's male naming tradition.)

At the time I was pregnant, Dave and I were living in West Virginia. After my first trimester I learned that my dear Aunt Maureen was sick with brain cancer. She had battled breast cancer years before and beat it, but cancer was back with a vengeance. Fear just shot through me, but I willed her to be well. I documented my pregnancy via videotape and mailed it to my aunt so she could see how I was progressing and know that she was in my heart and prayers. Never did I think she'd lose the second battle, but she did, only three months before my baby was born.

Heartbroken and devastated that my sweet, kind, fifty-three year old Aunt Maureen died, I hung up the telephone after hearing the news from my mother, and I dissolved into tears. Then I reached for the baby name book. Dave and I poured over the pages, determined to change the name of our baby to honor both my cousin Steve and my Aunt Maureen.

"What do you think of *Miranda*?" Dave asked, reviewing the "M" names.

"Shakespeare used that name in *The Tempest*," I said, always the English teacher. "It's pretty. Yeah, let's use that!" Then to honor my cousin we chose *Sophie* to go with *Miranda*, and *Miranda Sophie* became the girl's name. The boy's name would be *Matthew Stephen*. I called my mother who was at my Nanny's and Poppy's house with the Connecticut relatives, and I told her through tears that we were honoring my aunt and my cousin. I shared with her what the names of our baby would be. It meant so much to me to be able to give my grandparents and my heartbroken mother and other relatives some solace in that my aunt's spirit would be honored very quickly. It made me feel as if I was doing something when, really, nothing could be done but grieve the loss of a wonderful woman.

My mother's voice was pure emotion on the other end; she squeaked out, "Thank you, sweetie." Still on the telephone, she shouted behind her to those in the kitchen what the names would be, and I heard my grandfather let out a sigh of gratitude. His eldest daughter and grandson would be cherished in another new life.

I did not attend the funeral in Connecticut. I remember that April day standing outside on my deck in West Virginia, listening to the birds sing, smelling the sweet smells of spring, and just being heartbroken that someone so lovely was gone.

In August my daughter Miranda Sophie was born, and at her baby naming ceremony in the synagogue, she was given the Hebrew name Malka Shimona. My four grandparents and parents were there to witness this special, meaningful event that brought solace and happiness in a beautiful mixture into our hearts.

Now ten years later it's time to name another child. The name Crisna

Fernanda was assigned to her on her birth certificate. However, to us she is Lucinda Heather, Chaya Hertzaleah in Hebrew, named after Lillian and Harry, my mother's parents, who have since died.

What makes her name even more special is that I was able to tell Poppy that she was coming, that we were adopting her, and that she would be named after my grandmother who died five years before. And he was so touched. I could see a softness in his eyes when we said goodbye that final time. So now we honor his memory and accomplishments, too. Just like Aunt Maureen ten years before, my Poppy knew someone special was coming into the family whose names would honor our loved ones whom we miss.

Miranda Sophie and Lucinda Heather represent in life my cousin Steve, my Aunt Maureen, my Nanny, and my Poppy, and I smile, cherishing those beautiful people I loved and love whose memories are kept alive and poignant in the girls I cherish with all my heart. They are proof that life goes on. We remember and honor the past in order to give direction and shape to the future.

Chapter 7:

Time
January, 2003

It's amazing how you can start an average, typical day in the morning, and by the day's end, through a twist of fate, your life will never be the same again.

At 9:30 a.m. on a cold January morning in Massachusetts, Zadie drove Nana to a doctor's office for a routine check-up. After dropping her off in front so she didn't have a long walk to make, he maneuvered the car into the parking lot and walked to the office entrance.

He had done this hundreds of times.

But by 10 a.m., my grandfather's life as he knew it had already changed.

That is when my grandmother, worried that her husband didn't come into the doctor's office in a timely fashion, went outside to find him lying on the ground. He couldn't get up. She summoned help, an ambulance came, and both of my elderly grandparents were whisked away to the nearest hospital.

By day's end, after a battery of tests, there was a one-word explanation: stroke. My grandfather's right side was impaired. He couldn't walk. My grandmother went home by herself that night, something that hadn't occurred in over 60 years of marriage. She started her day going to her doctor's office, and my grandfather ended his day in the hospital.

Indeed, a twist of fate.

And while this was happening, Dave, Miranda, and I were celebrating the news that our adoption case that very morning entered Family Court in Guatemala City. While we were praying to God that Time would be kind to us and move mountains in its path toward quickly finalizing the adoption of Lucinda, my grandparents were praying that God would alter His plans just a bit and have Time slow down in order to let them have more time together.

Our prayers were fluttering up to God at the same time on the very same day.

When I heard the news of my grandfather's stroke, my heart, which moments before was full of joy and excitement, was broken. Time stood still. It didn't fly nor did it linger. It just paused to let me take a breath and think about the fragility and wonder of life.

I wanted Time to just get on its knees and crawl for my grandfather. I wanted my Zadie to get better, to get strength back in his right arm and leg, and to be able to resume his life again. I wanted my grandparents to be back together safely in their house and continue growing old together. I wanted my Nana not to worry. But I also wanted Time to soar so we would be able to bring into our family Lucinda.

A little baby is alive and well, living in Central America, not even knowing yet that her forever family is in North America and longing for her to join them as soon as possible. She is loved and so very much wanted.

My grandfather has been on this earth all the days of my life. Every day I have lived and breathed on this earth, he has been here, too. I can't imagine life without him.

Lucinda is three months old and will hopefully be with me on this earth for the rest of the days of my life. She doesn't yet know the tenderness of my voice, the gentleness of her father, the enormous amounts of love and affection her big sister is ready to shower upon her, and the joy she will bring to her extended family who cannot wait to meet her.

I can't imagine life without her either.

In the tapestry of life, I stand in the middle, the thread that overlaps these two vibrant colors.

In my mind I see my grandfather the last time that I saw him. He has soft skin with permanent smile marks embedded in his wrinkled cheeks, thick white hair that used to be dark brown like mine, a soft body that enjoys jogging suits and Velcro shoes as its uniform of choice, and sparkling, loving eyes that have witnessed a lifetime of family, friends, and moments to cherish and remember.

I gaze at the recent photo of Lucinda. She has soft velvet skin with two of the chubbiest cheeks imaginable, soft wisps of dark hair on her delicate head, a soft body that enjoys jogging suits and Velcro slippers as its uniform of choice, and sparkling, loving eyes that hunger to feel the love of family and friends and moments to cherish and remember.

My grandfather and my daughter-to-be are so alike. Another twist of fate…

I can't help but embrace Time and let go of the restrictions I try to place on it.

There will be time to love and to live. There will be time to grow and to strengthen, to nap and to rest. There will be sufficient time for everything.

And, with God's help, Time in the not-so-distant future will allow me to hold my newly-adopted daughter in my arms and introduce her to one of the most important people in my life, who, with gentle affection and tenderness that I've come to expect and love, will welcome her into the family of which he is patriarch. Their sparkling eyes will gaze at one another, marveling at the miracle of life.

And I will thank God for Time.

This is a photo of Leo Shore, my Zadie.

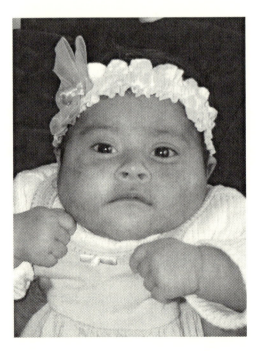

Lucinda at 2 months of age, December, 2002, in Guatemala; this picture was sent to us by our adoption agency.

Chapter 8:

It's A DNA Match

Last week we received DNA maternity test results from the American company Lab Corp. In Guatemalan adoptions, it is standard procedure for the birthmother and the child she is placing for adoption to have their blood tested to make sure they are a match. This is a United States requirement, because it ensures that the baby hasn't been stolen from his or her biological mother. Yes, sad to say, there are unscrupulous souls who kidnap babies and "sell" them. In our case, Lucinda and her birthmother have a 99.9% match, so this adoption is legal and will continue.

What is eye-opening is that on the report that was sent to us there is a grainy, black-and-white picture of Lucinda's birthmother Odelia holding Lucinda on her lap. This, again, is standard procedure, one more way to identify the birthmother and her child.

I can only imagine how Odelia feels, seeing and touching Lucinda.

On the forms Odelia had to use her thumbprint to sign her name; she is twenty-three and illiterate. It really hit home how much Lucinda's life will change when she joins our family here in the United States, and we are forever grateful for Odelia's decision to give her daughter a different life through adoption.

I notice on the paperwork that Odelia's birthday and my birthday both occur in the month of July. We share the birthstone ruby. In fact, Odelia's mother gave Odelia the middle name Rubi. So Dave, Miranda, and I have decided to change Lucinda's middle name from Heather to Rubi in honor of her birthmother. This gives Lucinda Rubi something very special from her past.

In the most recent photos emailed to us from the adoption agency, our

Lucinda is smiling. We are looking forward to the months to come when she will be home with us. When I look into her eyes, I melt. I already adore my daughter.

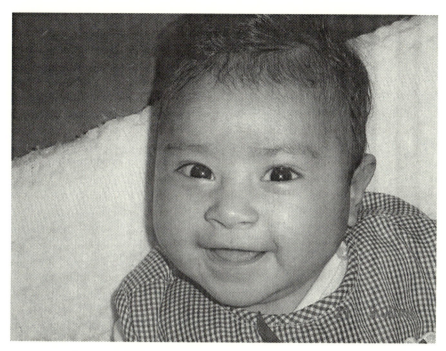

Lucinda, 3 months old; photo taken on January 21ˢᵗ, 2003, in Guatemala. For us, this is Lucy's first smile, and we are delighted to see it! I turn this into an 8 x 10 photo and frame it.

Chapter 9:

The Words You Don't Want To Hear
February, 2003

What does that mean, "The birthmother is missing?" I say into the telephone, my heart racing, knowing deep down that this is something that is going to rock my entire world to the core in about sixty seconds when it all sinks in.

I was told by my adoption agency that Lucinda's birthmother could not be found, and "they were out looking for her." The 'they' are the adoption contacts and the adoption facilitators who work with the Guatemalan lawyer on the case.

Translation: A contact is a local woman from the village who knows the pregnant woman (both are usually poor and uneducated). The pregnant woman goes to the contact to let her know that she wants to put her baby up for adoption. That contact gets in touch with the lawyer and tells him or her that she is in contact with a woman who wants to relinquish her baby. The contact is then "hired" as the "go-between." She makes sure information gets from the attorney to the birthmother and that all of the appointments necessary for the birthmother to attend are kept. It's a rather primitive way to conduct a 21st century adoption, but that is typically how it works in Guatemala.

So somewhere out there while I was on the phone hearing this disturbing news, there was a search going on in the mountains and villages of Guatemala to find Odelia, the woman who gave birth to Lucinda.

Why was the birthmother so important and necessary to the adoption at this point? Because in Guatemala, a birthmother has to sever her parental rights several times throughout the adoption process. It's not enough that she relinquishes her baby and signs papers. No, she has to have a DNA test to prove maternity (to make sure baby trafficking doesn't occur), then be interviewed by a Guatemalan social worker assigned to the case to say, yes, she really does want to relinquish her child, and then she has to again in another several months at the end of the adoption process sign away her parental rights in order that this child can be adopted by the family whose paperwork (remember that dossier?) has been thoroughly reviewed.

So it's a lengthy process for the woman who wants to ensure her child has a loving family and a promising future. It also seems to be a major slap in the face to her by the Guatemalan government who don't seem to really like international adoption but are forced to process adoptions because there are too many indigenous children born and not enough adopting Guatemalan families to care for them.

In a twist of irony, the middle and upper class Guatemalans tend to not adopt babies from the lower class.

So, without the birthmother, we cannot go forward with our adoption of Lucinda. If Odelia is missing, everything stops. I was told that, after a reasonable amount of time, if she is not found, then the baby has to go through an "abandonment" procedure. She will be taken away from her foster family (the only family she has ever known since she was two days old) and placed by the Guatemalan Court of Minors into a *hogar* (group home setting for orphans otherwise known as an orphanage) where she would most likely live for almost a year or more.

The Court of Minors will place ads in local Guatemalan newspapers and run announcements on radio stations, trying to locate Odelia's relatives with the hope that one of them will raise the baby. After several months, if the Court of Minors comes up empty-handed, they then declare the child "abandoned," and a Certificate of Abandonment is issued. The child is available for adoption *if* the Court of Minors believes he or she is adoptable (which means they will look at the age and gender of the children and only process those most favorable to adopting families). If the child is a two-year old male, for instance, most likely he will never be put up for adoption; he will live in the hogar until he is old enough to go out on his own. Translation: he will end up possibly being a homeless pickpocket or beggar or worse at the ripe old age of ten or eleven. Those most apt to be adopted after being abandoned in infancy are female toddlers, since most adopting families request baby girls.

It's a mess, if the birthmother is missing. And my heart was breaking into millions of pieces with this unfortunate news.

So began my time in hell when all I could do was wait and hope and pray.

Day after day, no, she wasn't found. "Do they have any leads?" I would always ask the agency's director and associates. The answers were always evasive. I never received any concrete information. I discovered that communication between the adoption agency and the adoption facilitators and lawyers in Guatemala City was weak.

At night I would lay awake, staring into space, wondering if our Lucinda would become *our* Lucinda, imagining all the twists her life could take if she had to go through abandonment.

I also thought about her birthmother. I just couldn't blame or hate Odelia. Poor, unmarried, uneducated, her life was unimaginably difficult. She gave the ultimate sacrifice by giving up her baby so her child would have a better life, but how long did *her* life have to be on hold for that to happen? Why couldn't Guatemala expedite the process in the best interest of both the birthmother and the baby?

Note that the birthfather has nothing to do at all with the Guatemalan adoption process. I guess adoption officials don't realize that "it takes two to tango." Women's lib hasn't seen its day yet... The burden is on the mother.

I was told that birthmothers often go into the mountainous areas to find employment if they can't find work in the villages (as migrant workers) or in Guatemala City (working mostly as domestics).

Sometimes the birthmothers connect with a new love interest, and she doesn't want him to know that she gave up a baby for adoption. If he were to find out, he might beat her. He might leave her. And in a world where you are hungry, tired, and scared, without any amenities and securities, that's not what you want. Everyone deserves love and affection.

The not knowing was the worst part of our ordeal. Would the birthmother be found? If she was found, would she agree to go forward with the adoption and be available for the necessary paperwork to sever her rights over and over again until the adoption was finalized and we could step in? If she wasn't found and Lucinda had to go through abandonment, would we be able to track her case and still adopt her down the road?

I never had a miscarriage with a biological child, but I felt the intense pain at this point in my 'adoption pregnancy'. I cried and cried and cried, thinking I was losing my child. At times, when I would think about all the unanswered questions and possibilities, I would lose my breath.

Mostly I ached for Lucinda, an innocent child who didn't do anything wrong but be born into a world that is so complicated. I wanted nothing more than to protect her in ways that I just couldn't. In my heart I was her mother, but in Guatemala, I was just a name on a piece of paper that linked us in someone's case file.

Dave and I didn't tell Miranda that Lucinda's birthmother was missing. We didn't want her to experience this pain. We didn't want to tell her anything until we knew what was going to happen. Even under duress, I can act well if it means protecting my child, and protecting her I had to do. I didn't want her to also be a victim of the crazy adoption laws that were causing us so much heartache.

I prayed for a miracle…

Chapter 10:

Not Meant To Be...But Why?
April, 2003

'Why?' was all I could ask, over and over again, still dazed by the devastating news from our adoption agency that Odelia was missing and our adoption was coming to an abrupt end. Why would a beautiful, innocent child be brought into this world, be placed for adoption so she could have a better life, be matched with a family who adored her even before they laid eyes on her, and then be forcibly taken away by "red tape" and illogical rules?

I was so angry. I just couldn't understand why God would allow this to happen.

During the weeks of not knowing what was going to happen to our baby, we prayed, contacted private investigators that we thought might be able to assist us in finding the birthmother (one gave me a $10,000 estimate to use his services with no guarantees), learned everything we could learn about Guatemala's abandonment procedures, and tried so hard to be patient.

But it was impossible to go through a normal day without feeling that pang in my heart that reminded me that all was not well in the world...*my* world in particular. With Iraqi War coverage blaring on the television and no leads coming in from Guatemala about the birthmother's whereabouts, my heart sank. I wanted to jump on an airplane and go to Guatemala City and find her myself, but that was just too ridiculous. Nevertheless, it crossed my mind a few hundred times.

We did call Guatemala one night in total despair and hired to help us a compassionate man named Manfred, a private attorney who specializes in adoption supervision.

I was desperate to make this right and have everything end happily ever after. But maybe that only happens in fairy tales. This is the real world.

Cruel things happen sometimes. For example, at the end of April the Guatemalan attorney hired by the adoption agency who is representing our baby told the adoption agency's director that Odelia had been found and she was willing to go forward with the adoption. When we got this news, we were elated! We could finally *breathe* again! I called the relatives and friends who knew about our ordeal, and they were thrilled! Our baby Lucy was, indeed, coming home!

But I thought it was strange that we could not get any answers to our questions about where the birthmother was when she disappeared. How could we make sure this didn't happen again?

Three days later she missed a scheduled appointment with a social worker in Guatemala's Family Court. Manfred called us with the news. Immediately I called our adoption agency and just fell apart on the phone. "I thought she was found," I said, over and over again. "What happened?"

A couple of days later, after the adoption agency did some poking and prodding for information (foreign adoptions are difficult in that information dribbles like a leaky faucet), we were told that the birthmother was not found. We deduced that the lawyer wanted us to hang on so he wouldn't lose his money that we sent when we accepted the referral; if we didn't know for another three months, he reasoned, who would it hurt? Maybe the birthmother would show up?

We were furious! We were heartbroken. The darkness came crashing down on us again.

It was time to tell our ten-year-old daughter. We avoided conveying this bad news to her, because deep down we really thought the birthmother would be found and then Miranda would be spared the anguish and pain. But we were told that the adoption would not go forward, that without the birthmother, Lucinda would have to go through abandonment procedures, and we would not be able to adopt her at this time. If we wanted to wait a couple of years, she may be available for adoption again, but there was no guarantee that the Court of Minors would put her up for adoption.

Miranda cried. Tears just streamed down her face, and I could see her anger and frustration when I told her what the outcome was. "What is going to happen to Lucy?" she asked, sobbing. I looked into her tear-filled eyes and told her that the Courts would ask Lucy's relatives to adopt her. Miranda did not ask me what happens if they said they didn't want to raise her; to her this child was irresistibly wonderful, so why wouldn't they? I was glad, because I didn't have the heart to go beyond that and tell her that the baby would have to leave her foster home and be raised in an orphanage.

"Are we going to adopt another baby, Mom?" Miranda asked, still crying. She so wanted to be a big sister. The daydreams we shared for so long felt so real. To think of a future without a baby in our family seemed very empty and cold.

"Yes," my husband and I said, nodding at the same time.

Sure, we were scared at the thought of starting all over again. What if lightening was to strike twice? Could our shattered hearts endure more sadness and pain? Were we crazy to go back into the uncertainty?

We couldn't think about all of that. We had to focus on our goal: to love and care for a child who needs a loving family.

Bad things happen. Life isn't fair. These are tough lessons that we three had to learn. It was a tough pill to swallow, but we did.

We don't know why this happened, what God intended, if this was fate or just a horrible tragedy, and we may never know. What we *do* know is that Lucinda will always be a part of our family and will forever live in our hearts.

Perhaps there is another Guatemalan baby not yet born who is meant to be ours. Despite the pain, we have to move forward.

Chapter 11:

My Letter To God

Dear God,

I know that I have so much to be thankful for. I have a wonderful husband who is hard-working, caring, responsible, and my very best friend. I have a terrific daughter who is healthy, loving, sweet, intelligent, and my very best friend. I am thankful for my extended family and friends who bless my life. I am thankful for the talents you've given me, the experiences I've had along the way, the teachers from whom I've learned so much, the sunshine and the daisies in the springtime.

You get the point.

So why can't I be Lucinda's mom?

When I first saw her picture back in November, my heart melted, and I was committed to that little girl, that sweet new life way out there in Guatemala. In that instant I *became* her mother.

And for months I watched her grow, and in my daydreams and in my conversations and mostly in my heart I saw her in my arms, I felt her soft cheek next to mine, I smelled the perfume of her new skin, I soothed her cries in the middle of the night, I reveled in her laughter, I took thousands of pictures of her beautiful smile.

She was to be Miranda's beloved sister, Daddy's little girl, my joy…

It seems as if in one horrible moment that picture of my family melted like watercolors on canvas. It was a shock that our adoption derailed and there was nothing in our power to get it back on track. Of course through the pain we were there for each other, comforted each other, loved each other when our hearts broke.

We are a family, a loving one. But it is as if someone is missing, and just like the proverbial elephant in the room that no one acknowledges, Lucy is everywhere I am.

Just this afternoon, the start of Memorial Day weekend, we three went to the movies to see *Bruce Almighty* in which actor Jim Carey becomes God.

Miranda asked me, "Mom, if you could be God, what would you do?"

In my heart I answered right away; there was no hesitation: "I would find Lucinda's birthmother so Lucinda's adoption could conclude the way it was originally intended."

But that's not what I said out loud to her.

No, I wouldn't ask for a million dollars, a book-publishing contract, or even to tame my wavy thick hair just once. But those are the things I told Miranda who seemed happy with my superficial answers.

A Guatemalan orphan whose birthmother is nowhere to be found, whose relatives cannot care for her, whose beautiful beginning is documented in our family photo album, who still lives and breathes in our hearts and souls – I have asked you, God, a thousand times to please give Lucinda the opportunity to come to the United States and be ours to love and cherish forever.

I'm asking yet again.

As an aside, did you happen to see that I shook the hand of the Governor of New Jersey this morning?

Covering a local story for the newspaper, I had the privilege to watch Governor Jim McGreevey read a children's book to second grade students at a local elementary school. I couldn't help but think, as he was talking with the boys and girls about dreams and how they come true, that if Governor McGreevey would make one simple call to one of New Jersey's Senators who would call President George Bush who would discuss our case with the President of Guatemala who would be willing to expedite an intensive search for Lucinda's birthmother who would be found and come forward and smile, saying, "Oh, I'm sorry! I thought my role in the adoption was over! Of course I will come back and sign the papers necessary to give my baby her family."

That would be a miracle... That would make my dream come true.

I am thankful, God, for so much. I know there are people in dire straights that need your immediate attention. But I just can't help but wonder why...why couldn't Lucinda's adoption happen the way they it was supposed to happen?

Why do we have to start all over again now with fear in our hearts and doubts in our thoughts?

Why can't Lucy be ours?

Please, God, continue to watch over Lucy and give her a beautiful, happy, healthy life. If she can't be with us, please make sure she has a family who will love her just as much as we would have ...as much as we still do... as much as I always will...

And please give me the strength to let Lucinda go, to say goodbye and not look back and forever wonder why...

Chapter 12:

When It Rains, It Pours
May, 2003

When it rains, it pours, but when you've been in a drought situation, you welcome the downpour. So it was one morning when I came home from driving Miranda to school to see a message from the adoption agency. "We have a baby! Please give us a call!" said Debbie, the director. It was 9 a.m. My heart beating a little faster, I called the adoption agency.

"Well, we have two baby girls with the same lawyer we want you to work with this time," said Debbie, "so we're going to send you the pictures of each and let you decide."

Two? That was unexpected... How could we possibly select a baby girl to be our daughter? I just shook my head... Just when I thought I was prepared for anything... Having lost Lucinda, we really were anxious and eager to love another little one again. But now there were two!

I walked downstairs, clicked on the computer, and waited for the pictures to download. Deep in my heart I was expecting, really hoping, to see Lucy again, and I must admit, my heart sank for a quick second when I saw a little face not Lucy's...

First appeared "Ana Marie," an infant with big eyes and pursed lips with a full head of hair going in a variety of directions! Next appeared "Andrea," a sweetie with big chubby cheeks, sparkling eyes, a full head of hair, and waving arms.

Oh, this wasn't going to be easy...

I gazed at each photo. Beautiful new little lives. So innocent. So vulnerable. So remarkably alive and full of energy. Personal and medical information on each would be coming in the next few days. A decision would be made then, and back on the merry-go-round we would go, this time desperately hoping that nothing would go wrong, that we would have a successful adoption and bring home a baby that would forever change our lives.

Today I was happier than I was yesterday. Today I smiled.

When I called Dave to talk about the photos of the girls that I forwarded to him at work, I heard optimism in his voice. We laughed about how big their eyes seemed in their little faces…

When I picked up Miranda from school, I told her about both babies and in the car showed her pictures; she, too, had a big smile on her face, but she worried that we wouldn't pick the "right one." I told her that God would send us signs that would help us decide, and she just nodded, most likely thinking her mom was a lunatic! Still, she was happy.

Tonight I will go to sleep not knowing which baby will be my daughter, but knowing that God is watching over us. Sure, He didn't allow us to bring home Lucinda, but there must be a reason…just as He brought these two beautiful baby girls to us this morning, the first day of May sunshine in weeks of April rain and gloom.

Life and death. Joy and pain. Life is mysterious, glorious, and ever changing. And this I know for sure: when it rains, it pours…so even if you don't have an umbrella handy, smile. A rainbow is coming soon to make it all worthwhile.

Chapter 13:

Making A Choice

Three days after receiving the referral pictures of two baby girls, the adoption agency called to say information was finally in on both girls. I sat down, pen in hand, ready to write important information. Surely there would be some sign from God showing me which baby was meant to be ours, and I was hoping I could decipher this divine signal as I scribbled words on the blank page. Something would surely push me in a direction.

Ana Marie, first.

She was born on May 21st to a nineteen- year old birthmother who lived in a remote village in Guatemala. The baby weighed six pounds four ounces at birth and all of her medical tests came back negative for disease. Hence, she was healthy and only seven days old…

Andrea, next.

She was born on May 12th at 3:20 a.m. in Guatemala City to a twenty-nine-year old birthmother who lives in the city. The birthmother is a domestic who most likely cooks and cleans for a wealthy family. Andrea was a whopping eight pounds, three ounces at birth and all of her medical tests came back negative for disease. She was healthy and fourteen days old…

Both girls were healthy. Now came the definitive contrasts that would set them apart.

Andrea was born first, and her birthmother lived right in the city, only one block away from the U.S. Embassy. Why is that significant? Because the birthmother has to sign papers several times in the coming months to complete the adoption. She is needed for the DNA test to make sure she indeed is the birthmother of this child, and then an interview with a Guatemalan social worker in Family Court is required. When the adoption file is released from the Guatemalan courts, the birthmother needs to sign papers severing for the last time her parental rights.

Knowing that the birthmother lives right in Guatemala City and has a housekeeping job is significant, because it will be easier for the Guatemalan lawyers representing the baby for adoption to locate her when she is needed to sign papers and appear in court. If the birthmother lives in a remote village outside of the city (Ana Marie's birthmother's situation), she most likely is a migrant worker in the fields; if she is in need of work when the season is over, she may be forced to go into the mountainous regions, disappearing from the lawyers who need to locate her for the adoption's completion. We could *not* go through that again.

Next, I looked at each birthmother's age. The adoption agency was told that Ana Marie's birthmother was only nineteen, but this was her second baby. Perhaps she had gone down the adoption road before. In Andrea's birthmother's situation, no information was given about prior children, but in a country that frowns on birth control (the Pope visited last year, emphasizing the Catholic Church's stand on contraceptives and abortion, perhaps the reason why there are thousands of Guatemalan children each year in desperate need of homes and families), she most likely has had other children. Yet it isn't known if either woman relinquished other children in the past. Surely one who did would know "the procedure" and be more reliable. That was my theory, anyway. I wanted to avoid at all costs the heartache we encountered in Lucinda's case where her birthmother vanished without a trace and we couldn't conclude the adoption. But in this case I wasn't going to know. Still, ten years of maturity *could* be a factor.

Birth weight… In Guatemala, babies are born smaller than babies in North America, mainly because the birthmother's don't eat as well nor do they receive state-of-the-art medical care as most pregnant women in the United States do. Andrea was eight pounds—big even by American standards for a newborn! Had her birthmother eaten well? Perhaps the family for whom she works fed her? Perhaps she lives with them?

Ana was six pounds…small but healthy. Both babies had their blood tested for a variety of diseases (including HIV), and both tested negative. The doctor who saw them in Guatemala was convinced that they were indeed healthy, vibrant little girls.

So that was all the information. Time to decide. The agency's Guatemalan lawyer asked that the decision on the referrals be made today so that both girls would be placed with families and their adoptions would begin as soon as possible.

"God, which one is meant for us," I thought, looking at the scribbles I made on the piece of paper in front of me.

Andrea was born first, and all along we were supposed to receive the first referral from the adoption agency. Andrea's birthmother would be the more reliable of the two, I assumed, based on age, location, and profession.

Andrea's chubby cheeks reminded me of Lucinda's... I so missed Lucinda.

Andrea was running away with my heart...

And with those deciding facts, I said, "We will go with Andrea."

Just like that. Decision made.

Another family was waiting for a baby girl, and the director was going to hang up the phone with me, and then pick it back up to dial their number. They had no idea that their baby girl was born and the information was on its way. Their hearts would leap and their daydreams would soar with that one phone call that was coming; that made me feel really good to know that both girls would have good families, good homes, and good lives. That was the plan, at least.

When I hung up the phone, I called my husband Dave at work to tell him the news. As I was talking with him, I opened the file on the kitchen table and gazed at the pictures of Andrea, *my* Andrea now. My heart did some flip-flops. Don't get too attached, I said to myself, my heart racing.

"Don't get too attached," said Dave, hearing the thrill in my voice.

And just like that, I grabbed the car keys and headed to the UPS store to send more adoption papers to the Guatemalan embassy and to the state department. It's 'hurry up and wait' time yet again...

Please, God, let Andrea's adoption be successful.

Chapter 14:

The Love of a Grandmother
June, 2003

My grandmother lives by herself now in the only house I've ever known her to live. My grandfather lives in a nearby nursing home where he moved after suffering a sudden stroke. My Nana and Zadie are so special to me, and I know how lucky I am to have had them by my side throughout my life. Some never get to know their parents' parents, but I have been extremely fortunate to know and love mine.

I am the oldest grandchild, making Nana and Zadie grandparents in their late forties. As a young girl, I used to walk the few blocks away from my house to my grandparents' house, trudging up their hill where their house sat at the top. Whenever I would arrive, my Zadie would have the biggest smile on his face, and within seconds, he would usher me into the kitchen where he always had something special for me. I was loved.

My grandmother and I used to do word search puzzles together, and she would marvel at how many words I could find, making me feel like a genius. We often watched soap operas together on TV and ate tuna fish sandwiches for lunch. One of the most vivid memories I have is when I was in the second or third grade and my bus used to drive past my grandparents' house on the way home from school. Almost every single day my grandmother would be outside at the end of her driveway, usually an apron tied over her clothing, and when the yellow bus would zoom by, she would wave to me, a big smile on her face. I was loved.

One afternoon I decided that I wanted to visit with Nana, and, I thought, "Why should I have the bus driver drive me home if all I was going to do was walk back over here to my Nana's house?" I asked the bus driver to stop at the top of the hill; having seen my grandmother wave to me over and over and over again for months, the driver knew it was safe. (Oh, how innocent those days seem now!)

That particular afternoon my grandmother was not at the end of the driveway, yet I knew where she'd be. My first cousin Laurie was just born, and I knew that Nana would be in the bedroom upstairs taking care of her. So I got off the bus and knocked on the door. Was Nana surprised to see me! "You better call your mother," she told me, holding the sleeping baby on her shoulder as she ushered me in the front door, "because she will be worried when you don't get off the bus."

I called my mom who, indeed, was VERY worried, and she made me call my dad at work rather than just give me the 'wait 'til your father gets home' warning. I knew I was in trouble! So I called my father who told me that I did a bad thing, that I didn't have permission and I worried my mother, and that I was going to be punished. I hung up the phone and my Nana held me close, telling me not to worry, all was ok; she said she would talk to my father. Now seeing that Nana was my father's mother, I had faith that she would be able to smooth things over. She was ever better than my mom in that respect.

Zadie drove me home. Then my father came home. The punishment: I couldn't go over to Nana's and Zadie's house for a month! Immediately tears sprang from my eyes, and I quickly dialed the rotary telephone in our kitchen. "Nana, Dad won't let me come over to your house for 30 days!" I sobbed. To me this was worse than no dessert or having to go to bed early!

"Give your father the phone," she said in a no-nonsense tone.

Well, let me cut to the chase... Nana saved the day, and I was able to visit her that weekend, but the bus driver was never again allowed to let me get off the bus at my grandparents' house without a note from my parents.

The next time I saw my grandmother she had a big can of black olives waiting for me in the kitchen. I put one on each finger and popped each one into my mouth! Zadie shared a hunk of kosher salami with me, the kind that is in an oblong loaf and was always a staple in his refrigerator. I had the best grandparents in the world!

I grew older and so did they. My Nana clipped out my articles when they appeared in the local newspaper. My Zadie took me to the Division of Motor Vehicles to get my driver's license. In fact, he was the first brave soul to get behind the wheel with me! Living with them one summer after my parents' moved out of state, Nana washed my clothes and Zadie let me drive his car when I worked as an intern at Apple Computer in the New England sales office. On Friday nights when my friends would come by the house, Zadie popped a big bowl of popcorn and brought it downstairs, a big smile on his face. They drove me to college on Accepted Candidates' Day, and even saw a rather risqué Greek play without flinching! After I was engaged to be married, Nana was the one who accompanied me to the dress shop to find the perfect wedding gown. And beaming with pride, my grandparents walked down the aisle and danced at my wedding.

When my daughter Miranda was born in West Virginia, my grandmother immediately asked me, "When can we come visit?" In their seventies, they jumped into the car and drove from Massachusetts to West Virginia, staying overnight at a hotel at my father's insistence; Zadie thought he could drive the entire way in one sitting, but we urged him to rest a bit. The baby wasn't going anywhere. In their trunk was a Mickey Mouse high chair. In their hearts was pure love and devotion.

Now in their eighties, they don't travel anymore; the long road trips are over. Instead, we drive to see them. And it's amazing to me that whenever I walk into their house, it's like I was just there. Besides the plastic covers finally coming off the velvet goldenrod living room furniture, nothing has changed. On the coffee table are jars of candies, on the tables are knick-knacks and frames, and on the walls are family photographs.

During my most recent visit, with great pain I told my grandmother about losing Lucinda. Always the great listener, she sat in her chair and nodded as I poured out my heart and soul. "It will be ok, you'll see," she told me, her eyes glistening. I showed her pictures of the new baby, Andrea, that we were trying to adopt. "Oh, she's beautiful!" cooed my grandmother who is now great grandmother to five.

"We're going to take things slowly and calmly this time; we're going to try not to be so emotional," I told her, my eyes belying my words.

"That's wise," Nana said, "but I think things are going to work out this time. You'll see," she said, confidently.

We went to the nursing home to spend the day with Zadie. I don't think he remembers that we're adopting a baby, but he sure remembers me. His eyes light up when he sees me walk through the door, and my heart melts when I see my dear old Zadie's eyes twinkle. Immediately he reaches into his pocket and gives Miranda three dollars in quarters that he won playing Bingo the previous day. I smile, remembering the dollar bills he always handed to my brothers and me, even though my father told him not to spoil us. Sure, Zadie is older, slower, and much more forgetful. But some things never change.

The next morning when I went to Nana's house to say goodbye, she was upstairs getting ready for her day's visit with Zadie. She goes to the nursing home every single day. While I was waiting for her, I happened to look at all the familiar things that remind me of my past. I noticed something new.

On the table was a small frame with a picture of Andrea inside it. It was near all the other great grandchildren's pictures. Overnight my grandmother took a bold step, a step that I was afraid to make, having been hurt once before.

Despite everyone else's warnings to protect ourselves from more possible adoption disappointments, my grandmother's loving gesture taught me something so profound: that life is meant to be lived today and that all one needs is courage, hope, and love to live well. One cannot be afraid to live or to love.

Every day my grandmother leaves her house to see my grandfather, to whom she has been married for sixty-four years, and every night she returns home, alone, to wash his clothes and prepare for the next day. Pictures in frames and the love of those whom she cherishes surround her now. She may be an old lady, but in her I see courage. I see faith. I will have courage and faith just like my Nana whom I adore.

There's nothing more special than the love of a grandmother...

My Nana, Lillian Shore.

Chapter 15:

Another Roadblock

It was 4 a.m. and I found myself staring at the bedroom ceiling. Rather than torture myself by tossing and turning in bed, I slipped on my slippers and headed downstairs to the computer. Writing always helps me sort things out.

So what's the problem? We hit another obstacle on our quest to adopt. This time it's red tape. Guatemala recently adopted the Hague Treaty that is supposed to facilitate and regulate international adoptions between countries. It seems as if some legislative authorities in Guatemala want to revamp the adoption program, centralizing adoptions like China does, and, in that respect, the government itself would coordinate the adoptions in the country, bypassing private attorneys, many whose livelihoods rely on adoption.

Late afternoon on Friday our troubles began. We received a call from our adoption agency; rumors were flying that the Hague Treaty announced on March 5th was going to temporarily suspend new adoptions. My immediate thought was, "Phew! Good thing our Power of Attorney document just arrived this week in Guatemala! Our case is active."

Oh no... That would have been way too perfect, don't you think?

It seems that our Power of Attorney was in Guatemala but in the translation process; once it was converted from English to Spanish, it would need to be registered with the Guatemalan court system in order to be considered activated. That would take a few days, and at that point Guatemala may not be activating new adoption cases. It wasn't known when that would change.

What happens to the children like Andrea who fall through the cracks of the old system and can't get their adoptions started under the new system? "No one knows right now," was the answer I received from our adoption agency's director.

So what changes are in store? Guatemala wants to establish state-run orphanages and abolish private foster care. They want one central authority to coordinate all adoptions. Besides psychological testing added to the dossier, they also want to make it mandatory that parents stay in Guatemala for fifteen days when they travel to bring their children back to North America. Right now the required stay is much shorter.

Most likely there will be more rules, and if our experience with Guatemala has been any indication of future expectations, we can conclude that these rules will be instantaneously made and enforced. Not enough manpower, finances, or resources? That doesn't matter. Guatemala does what it wants to do, and practicality doesn't factor into the equation. It's difficult thinking as a North American and dealing with a foreign entity. Most of the time there is no logic, rhyme, or reason to the process. But these are Guatemala's children and this is their program. My husband and I are trying to respect that.

Will we be able to go forward and adopt Andrea? We don't know. Once the Power of Attorney is ready to be registered this week, I will hold my breath and wait by the telephone to see if somehow we can slip into the system that is right now completely chaotic.

Do we move forward with Guatemala until they slam the door on us? Should we adopt a child from another foreign country? That would mean starting the paper process from scratch. Should we consider domestic adoption? We are not big fans of open adoption; the thought of selling ourselves in glitzy brochures to birthmothers doesn't sit well with us. Maybe we should try the biological route one more time, even if it means seeing fertility specialists this time around…

Should we jump off the baby carousel altogether? Is this dream not going to be realized? Is God trying to tell us something?

My head is spinning. I don't know what is going to happen, and the uncertainty is driving me crazy.

Chapter 16:

Fasten Your Seatbelt! Sharp Turn Ahead!

On our road to adopt, the pavement we traveled was riddled with potholes, big bumps, and several sharp turns. A recap:

First we accept a referral for Lucinda, then after several months her birthmother is missing and no one can locate her; we have to painfully let Lucinda go as her relinquishment becomes an abandonment in the Guatemalan court system.

Our innocence is shattered. We are afraid to move forward, but we do.

We receive two pictures of two baby girls and have to choose one to adopt. Trying to interpret God's signs, we accept Andrea's referral, gather all the necessary paperwork, and send it as quickly as we can to Guatemala.

Our attorney in Guatemala has trouble getting our dossier file out of family court, and it takes three weeks of constant checking until the judge finally releases it.

The week the Power of Attorney document arrives in Guatemala, the Guatemalan courts informally suspend adoptions as they restructure their adoption program. All adoptions after March 5th will have new rules and regulations, thanks to the Hague Treaty. Translation: more paperwork, more time, and more waiting on our part.

Rumor spreads that the adoption program in Guatemala is about to shut down. The U.S. State Department warns families not to adopt from Guatemala at this uncertain time.

And just as we think our dream of adopting is slipping away, that the adoption door is going to finally slam in our faces after all these months of hope and prayer, we get a call that will yet again cause us to swerve in a different direction.

3:30 p.m. Monday, June 16, 2003.

The phone rang and I saw on our caller ID that it was the adoption agency. I knew they would most likely be calling to tell me that they were not able to register our paperwork, that our adoption dream was going to have to be put on hold for an indefinite period.

I was ready, emotionally, for this final blow.

After much soul searching mingled with tears of sadness and frustration, my husband and I two nights before decided to end our eleven-month adoption journey. If we could not adopt Andrea from Guatemala, then it was time to stop. So much money and so many emotional ups and downs had finally taken their toll on us. Perhaps God was trying to tell us something, we reasoned. Perhaps we were not meant to adopt a child...

So when the phone rang, I was prepared to hear the bad news.

"Amy? I have some information for you," the director of the adoption agency said into the phone, "and I know it's going to confuse you."

"O.K. What's up?" I said, swallowing hard.

"Lucinda's birthmother has returned."

"WHAT?" I asked, afraid my ears were tricking me.

The director proceeded to tell me that, yes, the birthmother who had been missing since February came back to her village. No details were given as to why she left; no details were available about where she was all these months. But she was back. Our adoption of Lucinda could continue.

Needless to say, I was absolutely shocked!

"We need to know if you want to go forward with Lucinda's adoption," the director said when I was adequately convinced that I was not dreaming and this indeed was true. "We need to know if you would like us to place Andrea with another family who wishes to adopt a baby girl."

More decisions...

As much as we wanted Andrea to come home to be our daughter, our hearts months before had wrapped around Lucinda, the baby that God sent our way the first time, and we never recovered from the emotional scars her leaving created in our hearts.

I knew deep in my heart what we had to do.

Without any reservations whatsoever, I told the director we wanted to go forward with Lucinda's adoption. We had to get our dossier file back into family court (just days after struggling victoriously to get it released) and get Lucinda's birthmother into Family Court to see the social worker as soon as possible for her mandatory interview.

What if she leaves again?

We were told that the lawyer thoroughly explained to Odelia what was needed from her to conclude the adoption. She did return on her own accord, after all, and that was a good sign. But of course there were no guarantees. The adoption agency was going to see if they could help secure her a job in Guatemala City so they could keep a very close eye on her. And they were also planning to get a power of attorney document for her to sign after her interview just in case she was no longer in the village when the Guatemalan courts required her last signature at the end of the adoption.

Again, no guarantees.

I called Dave at work with the news, and he was dumbfounded. Miranda's eyes misted when she returned home from school and I told her about Lucinda. Her big smile mirrored Dave's and mine. We were afraid, but we were so elated, too! What was supposed to be a day of mourning lost opportunity turned into a reunion of sorts, a day miraculously filled with hope and so much possibility.

God sure works in mysterious ways. You never know what is right around the corner.

There is so much sorrow and heartache in life; when God throws you a great big beach ball of happiness, you have to catch it and tightly embrace it! And if tomorrow everything changes yet again, we at least had this day when our hearts were filled with joy and our eyes danced thinking of Lucinda, *our Lucinda*, coming home.

Chapter 17:

Manfred and the
Adoption Supervisors team,
My Guardian Angels In Guatemala

Everyone needs someone, and when times are rough, we look for those "guardian angels" who can help us get through the red tape and confusion that life sometimes brings our way. So is the case with Dave, Miranda, and me during this incredibly bumpy adoption journey.

Having lost Lucinda's referral because Lucinda's birthmother disappeared, then accepting Andrea's referral but not being able to have her case move forward because Guatemala's adoption laws were abruptly changing, we really considered throwing in the towel. So much hope and money had been invested in this dream of ours. So much time and energy and heartache resulted. But hope did still remain. And that was mainly because we found Manfred.

Servicios Juridicos Integrados, or Adoption Supervisors as their American clients know them, is a Guatemalan law firm headed by a man named Manfred and his partner Edwin that specializes in adoption supervision. Their "specialty" is rather new, though it is quickly illuminating the problems of adoption in Guatemala. American clients are flocking to Manfred (the only one in the firm who fluently speaks English) to help them get through the maze. But we are lucky in that we found him in his "early stage" of work.

Writing in February on the Guatemalan Adoptions computer listserv about our heartache regarding Lucinda's birthmother's disappearance, I received an email from an American woman in Antigua who provided me with the name of a "kind, generous" man whom she believed could help us in our situation.

At that point we were desperate, so what did we have to lose?

One evening after Dave came home from work, we sent Miranda upstairs to do her homework. Then Dave grabbed a phone and I grabbed another phone and we called this man in Guatemala, our first international call. Though he spoke with a heavy accent, his English was impeccable, and Manfred gave us the facts about corruption and adoption in his country. Could he locate Lucinda's missing birthmother? No. But what he *could* do was look at our file in Family Court and check dates and other important filing information that would shed light on our case. He could ethically talk to the attorneys, social workers, and judges involved. He said that sometimes the adoption agency's lawyers get nervous when he starts poking around their cases, and they "miraculously" find birthmothers who are missing or get adoptions moving when they were indefinitely stalled.

Dave and I looked at each other. We liked what we heard. So we hired Manfred's firm.

Our adoption agency wasn't happy we did this. This put pressure on them when their lawyers called to complain about his involvement. But did it put our case in the spotlight? Yes! And for once we were getting solid information, sometimes before the agency even got information about our case. Though our adoption agency seemed wonderful in the beginning of our adoption, their communication flaws and lack of decisive action made us feel hopeless. Adoption Supervisors changed that.

Every day Manfred sends me emails. He is faithful and loyal and incredibly driven. He told me that in the past he saw too many heartbroken families trying to adopt who kept bumping into walls when they would travel to his homeland to bring home their adopted children; he wanted to do something about that. He wanted to save the children relinquished or abandoned, get them into homes with families where they would be loved and cared for, protected and nurtured. He also wanted to expose along the way the corruption in the adoption system in order to eradicate or "scare straight" the crooked lawyers who give Guatemala a bad name. Instead of moving to Australia where he planned to retire, he decided to stay in Guatemala and follow his heart.

Manfred has a wonderful sense of humor. He likes to use smiley faces in correspondence and once reminded me that "my favorite Guatemalan" (as I affectionately call him) was still living in a Third World nation where sometimes during the rainy season the electricity goes out, explaining why I didn't hear from him the day before, a real rarity. When he has to tell me difficult news, he usually starts the email with, "My dear Amy…", softening the blow. And when there is good news to tell, he freely uses exclamation marks and bold font! This is not your typical, stodgy attorney.

As they started digging into court files, Adoption Supervisors were able to tell us a lot of details about our case. Manfred even uncovered some lies that we had been told. It was his sad duty to tell us when we needed to step away from Lucinda's case; he said that we could hire a detective, but other than giving out large sums of money, we would not be successful. According to Manfred, no one but the contact or the lawyer would be able to find her if she didn't want to be found. Because we trusted Manfred, we made the difficult decision to move on.

He is the one who told me to take some time to grieve. He is the one who suggested we take a break. He really cared. Those who don't live and breathe adoption don't understand the loss of a child, one you've never seen or touched, but one you love and dream about. Manfred really reached out and helped us acknowledge that loss.

Then when we received Andrea's referral, Manfred was filled with joy. He and his associates were ready to help us in any way that they could. We had to get into the court system, though, for them to begin their work.

And then, when all of our documents were ready to be entered into court, the Hague Treaty that Guatemala signed on March 5, 2003 derailed our efforts. Frustrated and disgusted with what he learned in court, Manfred ruefully told us one Friday evening that it might be time to look at adopting a child from another country. It would be anyone's guess what would happen in Guatemala, he said, and we could be setting ourselves up for much more heartache.

Then on Monday we got the incredible news from our agency about Lucinda's birth mother's return! I immediately wrote to Manfred, asking his advice.

"GO FOR IT!!!!" he wrote back, thrilled that we had another shot at adopting Lucinda; her case would fall under the "old" pre-March 5th adoption laws.

He called the Guatemalan attorney handling Lucinda's case over and over and over again, leaving messages when the calls were refused. He contacted the social worker in Family Court and made interview appointments for both the birthmother and the foster mother. We didn't celebrate until Manfred confirmed that, indeed, it was "looking good" that we were going to be successful this time.

Without Manfred, I don't know how we would have been able to get through all of this. God surely sent this wonderful man our way, and we are forever indebted to Manfred and everyone at Adoption Supervisors for their kindness and tenacity.

They are truly our guardian angels, and Manfred is someone I will always call 'friend.'

Chapter 18:

Waiting For The First of July

Lucinda's birthmother was back, but she had to stick around long enough to go into Family Court and talk with a new social worker assigned to the case. Odelia had some important papers to sign, and if she did this, we would be able to move forward with our adoption of Lucy. If she disappeared again, we would have to say goodbye to Lucinda, this time forever. The odds were 50-50, and we just prayed like we had never prayed before.

Back when everything looked hopeless and doomed, we decided we needed to get away, so we made plane reservations to Florida to visit my parents. And it would be during that week of sun and fun that I would have to be tenacious in my campaign to make sure Lucinda's birthmother was still around, was aware of her interview date set for July 1st, and that all of the "players" were ready to move forward.

Armed with the computer in my father's study, I emailed Adoption Supervisors and the adoption agency twice a day. I wrote "IMPORTANT" in the subject line, just in case the adoption agency might glance over it in search of important emails. Manfred was my cheerleader, telling me my "bugging" campaign was working, that the lawyers were daily reminded (by his firm and by the adoption agency) that the interview date was quickly approaching.

I telephoned the adoption agency every single day to make sure they were sending faxes and emails and telephone calls to their adoption facilitator who was the only one in touch daily with the attorney representing our case. Was the birthmother still in the area? Was she aware of the interview coming up? Did she know how important it was? Did the lawyer draw up a Power of Attorney document for her to sign after the interview? Did the agency have my parents' telephone number in case they needed to contact me? These were my constant questions all week.

The day we would be flying home was Tuesday, July 1st. Was this a good sign that we'd be up in the air at the same time that Lucinda's birthmother would be interviewed? What was God trying to tell me this time? I tried not to dwell on the timing too much. Instead, I would focus on the aftermath, getting home, clicking on the computer, and seeing Manfred's email, telling us whether or not the birthmother appeared earlier in the day in Family Court for her all-important interview. Everything was riding on that email.

Coming home from our last evening out at Miranda's favorite Italian restaurant, we heard the phone ring just as my father turned the key in the door; my mother rushed into the kitchen to answer it. "Amy, it's for you," she said. I was in the guest room, starting to pack. "It's Debbie," she told me with the phone receiver covered.

My eyes widened! Debbie from the adoption agency! Is the birthmother missing again? Is the appointment tomorrow in Family Court canceled or changed? Whatever it is, I bet it's bad news, I thought, taking the phone.

"Hello?" I said, waiting for whatever was wrong to clobber me over the head. "She did? Really?" I uttered next when I heard that the big appointment that we were waiting for had already taken place three days ago! And it was successful! The birthmother did show up and speak with the social worker, and the appointment is done. I couldn't believe my ears.

Our adoption of Lucinda was moving forward!

My parents, Dave, Miranda, and I were so happy! "It's really going to happen, Amy!!!" said my mom, hugging me. Of course until I heard confirmation from Manfred, I was still a bit on edge. But it was starting to sink in, finally, after all this time, after all these hurdles, after all these months... Lucinda was going to be ours.

Really.

Chapter 19:

We're in PGN!
July, 2003

After twelve months on this adoption carousel, we've learned a lot of new adoption lingo: *home study, dossier, referral, POA (power of attorney), bm (birth mother), fm (foster mother), sw (social worker),* and *fc (family court)* were just a few of the many terms and abbreviations that became a staple in our every-day vocabulary. Even Miranda was educating her friends in adoption-speak. Now we were happy to add the acronym PGN. Let me tell you why.

From the start, we knew that "entering PGN" was magical. Whenever a family entered PGN, they were ecstatic with the news and proudly announced it on the Guatemalan adoption listserv that we daily checked and rechecked online.

'We're in PGN!' was prominently displayed in the subject lines of these emails, and you knew you were going to either be very happy for this family (in the early stages of our adoption journey), brokenhearted (in the middle of our adoption journey when we were stuck in Family Court and Lucinda's birthmother was missing), or jealous (in the 'I can't wait any longer' mode of the adoption, when you see families who received their referrals after you somehow moving way ahead of you and, despite the rules of etiquette and maturity, you wish that it was you and your child in their place).

Anyone who knows anything about adopting from Guatemala knows the power of the letters P-G-N on hopeful adoptive parents. It's equivalent to Dorothy's excitement when she finally enters the Land of Oz after following that almost endless yellow brick road! Just when she thinks she is never, ever going home, she enters Oz. And for us that's PGN.

So what is PGN? Here's the simple explanation: first a family receives a referral, then DNA testing is done to make sure the baby and the birth mother are indeed related, the birth mother and the foster mother both are interviewed by a Guatemalan social worker, a report is written in Family Court; and all of those important documents in the dossier in addition to the social worker's move to PGN, the Procuraduria General de la Nación, which is equivalent to our Attorney General's office. This is the "last big stop" in the adoption process.

Guatemalan lawyers (called notorial officers) in PGN review each case with a fine-toothed comb. If there are typos, your case is "kicked out" of court until the documents are fixed. If your notary stamps on the dossier documents that you did months and months ago have expired, your case is "kicked out." Is the ink not dark enough on that signature? You guessed it—it may get "kicked out." (What are the rules, you ask? I'm still trying to figure them out…and so are the adoption professionals who work with PGN daily.) We pray that a very nice, calm, happy PGN attorney who is having a good day reviews our file. But that is rare. Most are very picky.

If your case gets "kicked out," you fix the document that needs fixing (which sometimes takes weeks, because you have to start from scratch, and do all that state department-embassy authentication business that you did months ago when you first prepared the document for the dossier), and then your lawyer resubmits the file back to the PGN lawyer. That is called going "back in." Sometimes your file can get kicked out, put back in, get kicked out again, then put back in again, and so on, and so on, because the PGN officer does not look at the entire file in one sitting. When he/she finds an "error" (typo or incorrect birth date—they all carry the same weight in PGN), he/she immediately "kicks out" the file. So when the lawyer puts the file back in, the PGN officer then continues through the file. I think you get the picture. This is very frustrating, nerve-wracking, tedious, tiring, and time consuming.

When everything is flawless (which could be in just a couple of days or several months), a judge approves the paperwork in the file, and that is when you "exit PGN." Exiting PGN is totally amazing, because that signals the "end" of the adoption journey. After that, the birth mother relinquishes her maternal rights for the final time, and a new birth certificate for the child is issued. The adoption is then final!

With that said, let's get back to our case…

It was midnight *again*, and I couldn't sleep *again*, and I slipped on my slippers and headed downstairs *again* to check my email *again*.

I was waiting for an email from Manfred that told us we were "in PGN." I never thought I would ever hear those beautiful letters and our case in the same sentence. I just kept thinking that something else would go wrong. We got "stuck" in Family Court for five months, and it felt as if we were never ever going to progress from that step in the process.

But we did!

"On July 8th your case was filed and entered into PGN," was the message Manfred sent me. He added an exclamation mark and a smiley face, knowing how this news was going to make me feel. (At this point, we were great pals.) *We're in PGN! Oh my God, WE'RE IN PGN!*

It was dark, Dave and Miranda were sound asleep, and I was sitting downstairs in front of the computer with the biggest smile on my face. So I started to write an email, with 'We're in PGN!' in the subject line.

FINALLY it was *my* turn!

Chapter 20:

Hellos and Goodbyes...

The months either crawl by, day by day, moment by moment, as if I'm staring at the clock and willing each second to move faster than a snail or they fly by in a whirlwind, and I am shocked when I look at the calendar and see where we are, today, and where I was the last time I glanced at the calendar.

It's "waiting for Lucinda" time. Last summer is when we decided to adopt, and now one year later we're still waiting. It seems so long ago when we filled out our first form, but it feels like yesterday, too, if that makes any sense.

Since making the decision to bring Lucinda into our family, the following has transpired:

Poppy died of heart failure.

Zadie had a stroke and moved into a nursing home.

The United States sent troops to Iraq to liberate the people from Saddam Hussein.

My younger brother Jon and his wife Melissa became parents in February to Matthew, my only nephew.

My younger brother Dan and his wife Abbie became parents in May to Jessica, my only niece.

My mother's beloved cat Penny died at the ripe old age of twenty-one, leaving my mother heartbroken; one month later, she went to an animal shelter and adopted Sunny, a one-year old gray cat who instantaneously brought so much joy into her heart.

My in-laws survived another snowy winter in New Hampshire.

Miranda completed the fifth grade.

Dave's Aunt Vilma died after a seven-week battle with lung cancer.

It was the last item in that list that had us abruptly packing our bags and heading for Massachusetts to attend a funeral.

It was a somber, gray, July morning, unusually chilly for summer in New England, and on that day Aunt Vilma, seventy-two, was remembered for her kind heart and loving ways. Family gathered from different corners of the country to come together to say goodbye to one of their beloved.

Its days like these when you realize how important family is. In the hustle and bustle of living life, we are stopped in our tracks by death, a reminder that we are not permanent fixtures in this world, that we sincerely belong to those who love us. Those who need reassurance that life is worth living sometimes need us to remind them of that.

And just as quickly as we came together, we parted ways to return to the lives we temporarily interrupted, yet this time a little more sober and reflective. Instead of darting back to New Jersey, we spent the next day and evening with my grandparents.

Anytime I walk into my grandparents' house, I'm transported to yesterday, when I was younger and life seemed so magical and lazy. It seemed back then that my birthday took forever to come around again, and sometimes I just didn't believe that I really would be grown up some day. There was my grandmother, waiting for us, a big smile on her wrinkled face. After hugs and kisses, we headed out to the nursing home, my grandmother's new home away from home, to see my grandfather. And after several months of living in the home, I even return to these hallways with a warmth in my heart, knowing that when we go up the elevator and turn the corner, there Zadie will be, waiting for us.

And, like magic, my eyes land on the short, white-haired man with the smile on his face. His mind may not be as sharp as a tack anymore, but he remembers us. It's as if the clock starts ticking when he sees my grandmother's face in the mornings, since that moment is the reason he eats and breathes every day. It's an added bonus when others he knows and loves accompany her. We spend the day talking, listening to Miranda play the piano, watching the flowers blow in the summer breeze outside on the patio where we enjoy some fresh air. Life is slow and tranquil in the nursing home.

After we say goodbye to my Zadie for the evening, we take Nana to a restaurant for dinner. We talk about today, yesterday, and memories of long ago. Before long, it's time to say goodbye to Nana who waves to us from her front door just as she has waved goodbye to me from that door my whole life.

One more goodbye…

Heading home to New Jersey, the three of us are quiet, each reflecting on the weekend in our own way. Somewhere after hour two of the five-hour journey, we start to settle back into our present and drift away from our past.

By hour three, we are fully absorbed in the book on tape that we're listening to in the car. We start to rummage around for the bag of snacks that we have to keep hunger at bay. By hour four and one half, we start to perk up, seeing the familiar sights and sounds of home.

And then, after five long hours behind the wheel, Dave pulls the car into its designated spot, and we're home. Miranda heads over to the mailbox to get our mail, and she squeals with delight when she notices an envelope from the adoption agency. *"Pictures, Mom!"* she says, showing me the envelope that elicits big smiles from Dave and me. This was the first time we were getting to see pictures of our Lucinda since her birthmother disappeared several months ago.

Drop the suitcases! Drop the bags! Drop the rest of the mail on the floor!

The three of us instinctively head to the couch. On my left is Miranda; on my right is Dave; I sit in the middle. Opening the envelope from the adoption agency, I reach in and take out a stack of pictures, and we hungrily gaze at each one. There, in front of our eyes, is Lucinda, now nine months old, sitting pretty in a pink lacy dress. Her face is so serious. She doesn't smile. But it's our baby Lucinda, all right. We see the same features, now more defined, in the face that we adore. She is sitting on her own. Her eyes are big brown saucers. Her hair is curly, thicker than before. And her cheeks are still chubby, flawless, with those soft pink lips in the middle of her face.

We outwardly smile. We inwardly ache. We seem to keep saying hello and goodbye and hello and goodbye to those we love. But we hang on for the next time we meet again. It's always worth it, no matter how long the wait.

Lucinda, 9 months old, sitting on a hotel couch in Guatemala.

Chapter 21:

Do You Think I Can Lift Her?

Miranda turned eleven on August 13th, and we started our celebration that day by going to the mall and shopping. We headed straight for the cosmetic jewelry boutique to buy dangling earrings (Miranda's favorite since she got her ears pierced last year), then darted right over to Gap Kids for serious clothes shopping. Every kind of denim imaginable was on the racks, so we selected as many pants as we could carry in Miranda's size and wormed our way to the fitting room. Each pair delighted Miranda as she posed in the mirror to review her "look." We made the difficult decision of narrowing the selection down to an affordable purchase, and then headed outside again to take one more look around the store. Miranda and I are serious bargain hunters.

Satisfied that we bought enough clothes to make my daughter look cool and feel comfortable in sixth grade, we got in line at the cash register. While we waited, we saw several infants and toddlers in strollers, their mothers shopping in the baby section. I saw the spark in my daughter's eyes when she saw a baby looking her way and then smile at her. There's nothing more special than a baby's big grin! And Miranda's face delights in the innocent love coming her way.

Now when she sees babies and toddlers, Miranda has a "vested interest" in them since she is patiently, sometimes agonizingly waiting for her baby sister to come home to us. She points to the babies she sees, and we smile together, adoring with our eyes their chubby cheeks and cute outfits. "Mom, she's soooooooooooooooooo cute!" whines Miranda with a big grin on her face. I know that she would love every single one of those babies if I told her that indeed that was the one we were adopting! She yearns to hold them and teach them all that big sisters teach little ones. And I tell her to be patient, that one of these days it is going to happen.

Our eyes lock and we squint with love, knowing the ache we each feel inside, wanting to make that moment happen sooner than later. We each think that maybe today's the day that the phone will ring, giving us the good news. But then we warn ourselves that it most likely won't be the day, so we won't get our hopes up. But maybe…maybe not…but maybe… This is how we've been thinking all summer long.

After making our purchases, I hand Miranda the giant Gap bag for her to proudly carry out of the store. "Is it too heavy for you?" I ask, but she looks at me like I'm crazy, shaking her head no.

"I can carry it, Mom! I'm not a little girl, you know!" my pre-teen reminds me, lugging the bag. I see her straining a bit, holding the bag up awkwardly so it doesn't drag on the floor, but I pretend not to notice. "Do you think Lucy will be this heavy?" she asks. This is a question I hear often.

When we are at the grocery store, Miranda likes to pick up jugs of apple juice and ask if Lucy is that heavy. She cradles the jug in her arm as you would cradle a baby, and I can't help but smile. It's so sweet. She does the same to bags of cat litter and laundry detergent containers. If you were to ask Miranda what she really looks forward to when her sister comes home, she will tell you, without hesitation: she wants to hold her and carry her everywhere. In fact, when we purchased a stroller a few months ago, Miranda thought we were crazy to waste the money, because she said she would carry Lucy everywhere. "I will carry her through the mall and in airports and in the neighborhood and she will sit on my lap in restaurants," my daughter tells my husband and me matter-of-factly. "She won't be in that stroller if I'm around."

It's going to be hard for Lucy to actually get on the floor and learn how to crawl and walk, because we have almost a year of kisses and cuddles and hugs to make up for her year away from us. Something tells me that Lucinda is ready for all the love and affection we can shower on her. And we are more than ready, too.

When Miranda asks me, "Do you think I can lift her?" I always respond, "Yes. Don't worry." And I can't wait to see my older daughter holding my younger daughter in her arms. Will it be tomorrow? Next month? Next year? I don't know, but when I close my eyes, I see that picture, and that's what keeps me patiently waiting.

Miranda, age 11.

Chapter 22:

Labor Pains

Labor Day is here. It's the official end of summer. Temperatures are cooling down already, and every now and then I see a leaf or two flutter to the ground. It's time to transition into a new season.

Miranda starts sixth grade next week. Life gets more harried and hurried as we try to keep up with our scheduled commitments that were on hiatus during the summer months. It's as if we have to officially take off our flip-flops and lace up the Nikes; time speeds up again.

And the fact that we're moving into a new season and a new phase of life saddens me, because we are STILL WAITING for Lucinda.

Ever since November when she digitally jumped into our hearts from the computer screen, Lucinda became a part of our family, an important part. So every single day, some time, some way, we have thought about her. With every email, photo, phone call, INS notification, notary stamp, UPS delivery, and dream, she has been with us.

Prior to summer when I made plans to join the pool club in our town, I asked about the baby policy, knowing our little girl would be coming to the pool with Miranda and me daily. I could imagine those little arms splashing water, those beautiful dark eyes sparkling in the summer sunshine, that smile melting my heart. I was tempted to purchase a bathing suit for her—all the little girl suits were just so precious on the little hangers—it was hard to resist. But I did. However, I did buy a little yellow floppy sunhat. I had to. I figured that had a longer life than a bathing suit JUST IN CASE THE BABY WASN'T HOME IN THE SUMMERTIME.

Way back then, it seemed impossible that she wouldn't be home by June. Then we had all those twists and turns. Now it's practically September, and we're still waiting for our baby girl. We went from autumn to winter to spring to summer and back to autumn…and we're still waiting.

I know what makes the waiting so unbearable. It's the dreaded fear that all of this is a dream. Without concrete verification that we WILL DEFINITELY have Lucinda home with us some day, we are gripped with the fear that maybe we won't. Don't forget, we once traveled down that road. And just the thought that Lucinda may not come home to us makes my head spin. It's something I can't think about, can't verbalize, and can't acknowledge as a possibility, because if I did, I would cry a river of frustrated tears.

It's just not fair that we adoptive families have to wait SO LONG to bring home our children. We've gone way past the nine-month mark; our hard labor has to have an epidural come to the rescue! It's just agonizing and difficult to describe to anyone who hasn't walked in our shoes.

My mother tells me to believe. "It's going to happen," she says. My father asks for daily updates. "It won't be long now," he predicts. "What's going on with the adoption?" Everyone who knows us asks that question. To those who haven't seen me in a few months, they are SHOCKED when they see me out and about these days without a baby in tow. I cringe when I see on the calendar that my six-month dental appointment is nearing. The friendly dental receptionist looked shocked the *last* time I was in without a baby in my arms! Even Miranda's friends can't quite understand what the problem is. "If you want to adopt a baby who doesn't have parents who can care for her, who lives in another country, you simply fly to that country and bring the baby home," they think.

Oh, if it was only that simple. And why shouldn't it be? That is what keeps me up late at night, wondering why this is all so complicated.

Until we actually get "the call" that tells us we are out of PGN and approved by Guatemala to adopt Lucinda, all we have to cling to are pictures and reassurances and email updates on our mounds of paperwork. And all those dreams.

We are already a family of four. Miranda is already a big sister. Dave and I are the parents of two girls. My parents and Dave's parents count Lucinda as one of their grandchildren. My grandmother tells people she has a great granddaughter in Guatemala. Lucinda is always talked about, always mentioned, always a part of our telephone conversations, family get-togethers, and holidays. She is an integral part of our daily lives.

But she's still not here.

And the waiting is getting unbearable…

Like a very, very pregnant lady who just doesn't think that baby in her protruding belly, now almost a week overdue, is ever going to come out into the world, I'm ready to push really, really, really hard...

It's Labor Day.

I feel labor pains.

It's time.

Chapter 23:

Me And My Fat Black Cats

Every day since seeing her beautiful face on my computer screen last November, I have thought about Lucinda upon awakening to start a new day, and every evening before I close my eyes to sleep I say a little prayer that Lucinda will be home with us soon. And in all that time, I've started to look for "signs." Surely God is listening, I tell myself. Every now and then something happens that proves I'm right. Is it just coincidence or am I divinely inspired? I don't know. But I'm not taking any chances.

Back in my early twenties, I got married and moved from Massachusetts to West Virginia. It was culture shock, to put it mildly. And helping me through that transition was my mother. When I was growing up, my mother and I were close. However, having two younger brothers always created challenges. I wanted my mother's attention more than I got it, I recall, but once I grew up and got married and my brothers left the nest to embark on their own independent lives, my mother and I were able to resume that special mother-daughter relationship.

But now miles and miles separated us. Not the adventurous type, my mother only traveled by plane with my father. Because he ran his own business, it wasn't that easy for him to get away, and my mother and I both knew that meant it would be few and far between when we would get to see each other. That is, until my mother got hit with the 'I am woman, hear me roar' bug! From that point on, life was never the same.

Mom decided that she was going to get on a plane in Boston, Massachusetts and fly to Pittsburgh, Pennsylvania, make a connection, and then fly into Charleston, West Virginia all by herself. She loved me that much. I'll never forget waiting for her, standing in front of one of two gates in the little airport that makes Logan International look like a giant, waiting for her. And then suddenly, like in a dream, she appeared, holding a carry-on, a big smile on her face. I could tell she was so relieved to be at her destination, proud that she did it successfully on her own, and overjoyed to see her first born! We hugged each other, and in my mother's arms, I felt like I was home again.

We talked until we were hoarse, and we did a lot of shopping on that visit. One of the trinkets that I retain from that time is a pair of earrings. My mother and I were browsing a department store when we came across these beautiful enamel earrings, all in the shape of colorful cats! Being cat aficionados, my mom and I were so excited to come across this find. We poured over them. Mom wanted to buy a pair for her and a pair for me, a reminder of our special time together. In the end, I selected a pair of fat black cats outlined in gold and my mother chose a pair of bright red cozy felines. From that day on those earrings became my absolute favorite possessions in the entire world.

Long after my mother returned to Massachusetts (and what a tearful goodbye that was), I wore the earrings religiously. They reminded me of my mother, and they made me feel protected, safe, secure, loved, and close to home.

As the years went by and I went from a green twenty-something to a more confident thirty-something, now living in New Jersey and a mother myself to Miranda, I started changing my earrings. After all, variety is the spice of life, right? I couldn't wear big fat black cat earrings every single day forever and ever. I wanted to be fashionable, so I bought gold dangling earrings, hoops, and other dramatic, sophisticated styles. I still adored the earrings that my mother bought me, but they were in my jewelry box, retired.

That is, until Lucinda's birthmother disappeared. And when that happened, I was devastated. I wanted so much to adopt Lucy, and it didn't look good that that was going to become a reality. Those 'bad' days I didn't wear any jewelry, any make-up. Who cared? There were more important things in life to worry about. I grieved for the loss of a precious gift that God for some reason took away from me.

And that's when I started to pray every day. I think God and I had a good relationship before this, but I didn't feel the need to 'check in' with Him on a daily basis. But when I had nowhere else to turn, when my mind was speeding out of control and my heart was breaking, I started to talk out loud to God. And it made me feel better. Slowly I came back to life, with a few important changes to my daily routine.

Off went the dangling earrings, and on went the big fat black cats. That same source of comfort and love that I felt back in West Virginia when I felt lost gave me strength again. I also started to wear the Star of David necklace I bought in Israel when I was sixteen, traveling on my own for the first time. I figured it would literally and figuratively keep God close by. And I talked to my mother every single day by phone. These days, she's now living in Florida with my dad, and we're still maintaining a close long distance relationship.

These changes empowered me to feel confident, and with Dave I was able to make decisions in the adoption process that had to be made. Months later when I finally let go, knowing God works in mysterious ways, telling my mother that there must be a reason for everything, I moved on. And that is when the phone call came telling me that Lucinda's birthmother returned and was ready to go forward again with the adoption. My prayers were answered!

Since then, I religiously wear my fat black cat earrings and my Jewish star. Whether I'm wearing shorts and a t-shirt or a skirt and blouse, these are my staples. Superstitious have I become? Maybe. I know, certainly, that these material objects aren't the reason for good luck to come my way, but they make me feel good about myself. They make me feel protected, confident, like I can face anything. Symbolically I carry my mother in my head and God in my heart, and with that combination guiding me through life, how can I go wrong?

Chapter 24:

Are We 'In' Or Are We 'Out'?

The bad news: we were "kicked out" of PGN three weeks after our adoption attorney submitted our case file to PGN. The PGN attorney assigned to our case wanted more documents that included the birthmother's birth certificate, the birth mother's cedula (which is equivalent to our social security number), and an updated medical report on Lucinda. Since all that falls on the Guatemalan end of the adoption process, we had to sit and wait until the attorney gathered these documents.

The good news: our case was resubmitted to PGN two weeks later.

The fourteen days and nights we spent out of PGN we classify as "wasted" time, because our case was not going forward until it got back into the system. So we were happy when we were told we were back "in." Again, we waited (in the "bad" way) two weeks to be told we were back "in," and then the "good" wait began again. (Anyone I try to explain this to thinks I've lost my marbles!)

Then, three weeks later, we held our breath and....................we were told that we were kicked out again, but by the time we were told we had been kicked out, our attorney resubmitted our file with whatever the PGN attorney requested, so we were back in by the time we found out that we had been kicked out for the second time. (Are you following me?)

Another couple of weeks went slowly by, and just when I thought we were about to get "the call," that surely the PGN attorney had approved our case and the judge was ready to sign off, we received an email from Manfred that (sigh) we had been "bounced" again from PGN.

Because Adoption Supervisors was taking advantage of the long weekend (Guatemala's Independence Day) and closing their office on Wednesday to do some rewiring, I called our adoption agency and asked them to look into why we were kicked out of PGN a third time.

I have to admit, my patience was unraveling. I was so disappointed hearing this news. And it came right on Dave's birthday. In my mind, I fantasized that since Dave's birthday was coming, surely God would coincide the good news about Lucinda's adoption so we would have an even bigger reason to celebrate! It didn't happen.

The strange thing is this: the adoption agency's director said she would look into it and call me back. She telephoned the adoption facilitator in Guatemala, and, after checking with the attorney and PGN, she learned that we were still in PGN, that there had been no change at all! This was Thursday. I asked the director to ask them to check again on Friday. Things work slowly in Guatemala, and Manfred was always right.

I of course wanted us to still be "in," but if, indeed, we were "out" it was important for us to know why so we could fix whatever needed fixing in order to get us back "in" as soon as possible. If our case was still in the court system, we had to hurry up so we could continue to wait the 'good' wait!

Again, on Friday, I was told that our case was still in PGN.

So that's how we started our weekend. "Are we in or are we out?" was the question. At this point, Dave and I had developed a warped sense of humor and a thicker skin in order to deal with all the disappointments and delays with the adoption, so we were able to laugh about our quandary. It was going to be another night of sleeping with uncertainty.

The good news: Saturday morning we got a great surprise—new email pictures of Lucinda! We three crowded around the computer screen as I downloaded the images of our now ten and a half month old beauty! This time Lucinda was sitting on a chair outside a white stucco building somewhere in Guatemala. Her curly hair was blowing slightly in the breeze. She wore a short sleeved, velvet dress with a lace color, lacy white socks, and black, shiny shoes. The greatest surprise of all was when we downloaded a picture of our baby smiling! Her eyes crinkled, we knew as the picture appeared from top to bottom slowly on the computer monitor that a smile was coming, and we were so excited! We only saw one smile before, and that was when Lucy was almost four months old.

Miranda and I wondered out loud what her little voice must sound like. Dave wondered out loud if she was crawling or if she had any teeth yet. We just gazed at her photos and smiled, for a brief moment feeling joy and contentment knowing our baby was healthy and happy. In those shining minutes we forgot about the wait and just let our hearts and eyes dance with joy.

After printing the pictures (to gaze at over and over and over again throughout the weekend), I noticed the digitized date on them. I realized the photos were taken the day before at 11:00 a.m. I thought about what I was doing at 11: 00 a.m. It's magical to think that Lucinda and I are both in this same world, simultaneously living, though we are so far apart. And then I was touched to see the time stamp on the email. The adoption agency sent the photos to me at 11:00 p.m. They knew how anxious we were to see our baby, and it meant a lot to me that they took the time to get the photos to us as soon as possible. They could have waited until Monday, but they didn't. That's a little detail that means so much.

Sunday morning we headed to our synagogue. Miranda was starting another year of Hebrew School, and we were attending another religious school parent meeting. Of course, we were asked at least four or five times before the meeting began, "Where's the baby?" and "What's taking so long?" I wanted to kick myself for telling so many people, because every time we get asked those questions, we hurt. We were internally asking these same questions every moment of every day. And to have to verbally explain it over and over again, well, there's only so many times you can say "yet another delay" before you feel like a broken record.

And in the eyes of our friends and acquaintances when we say YET AGAIN "it should be any time now," we imagine that we see a fleck of doubt in their eyes, that they are starting to think, "Hmmm, maybe this is NOT going to happen after all. Poor Amy and Dave..."

Then again, maybe that's our doubt creeping in, making us paranoid. Whatever it is, Dave, Miranda, and I feel tied together in our sadness, united in our hopefulness, and just plain old frustrated by the whole experience.

Monday: Happy Independence Day, Guatemala! All courts and embassies were closed on September 15th for the holiday. We still had a twenty-four hour wait until Manfred could answer the question, "Where are we?"

So before the computer I sat and gazed at the new photos of my precious younger daughter, feeling the joy and the pain intermingle in my heart. I wanted to hold her, wanted to bring her home, wanted to hold her little hand and hear her little voice. I was delighted in seeing her smile. I gazed into her eyes that looked straight into the camera for another monthly "photo shoot."

Are we in or are we out?

What's taking so long?

Tune in tomorrow...

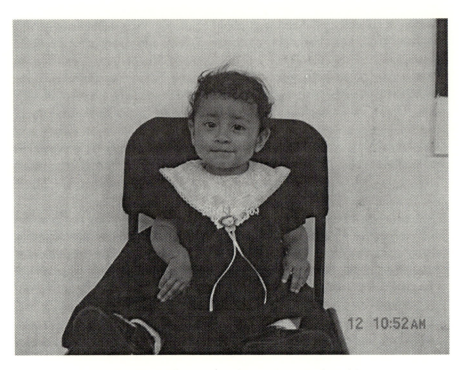

Lucy, September 12th, almost 11 months old.
She is outside somewhere, the breeze blowing her wispy hair...
I love the little smile on her face, and I yearn to hold her.

Chapter 25:

Eternal Spring

During the long wait, I decided I had to focus my attention in a positive direction. So I decided to learn as much as I could about the country of Lucinda's birth. Guatemala is known as the "land of eternal spring," because their temperatures are always mild. From pictures, I see lush greenery, beautiful mountains, and serene lakes. Of course, that is in the travel brochures. If you are one of the indigent, life in Guatemala most likely is not so lush, even with that gorgeous backdrop in place. I've seen the mud huts, the communal watering holes, and the shoeless children when I research deeper into the land of my second daughter. Guatemala is a land of contrasts for the haves and have-nots.

International adoption certainly changes the lives of thousands of children each year who leave behind their Latin American birth countries and culture and venture into wealthier lands with parents who can afford food, clothing, shelter, and educational opportunities for them. But that doesn't mean it's right. I have mixed emotions, really, about international adoption. When I think about how drastically different Lucinda's life will be with us versus how it would have been with her birthmother, I can't help but think of that awesome responsibility we all have, as parents, to shape the lives of our children.

One thing that will remain the same: the lush green backdrop. Dave, Miranda, and I painted Lucinda's bedroom walls a lush green color in honor of Guatemala, the Land of Eternal Spring.

As one who tries to learn as much as she can about Guatemala's culture, I stumbled across a site on the Internet called Mayan Traditions. This is a Fair Trade project, meaning a fair and equitable partnership was made between the marketers in the United States and the producers in Latin America. This type of partnership greatly helps the poor, struggling Guatemalan artisans and farmers. There is a Fair Trade Federation that monitors these projects, ensuring that a fair wage is paid, that employees have opportunities for advancement, that even the most disadvantaged are provided equal employment opportunities, and that healthy, safe working conditions are met.

I was drawn to the Mayan dolls, and that's where I clicked my mouse. "Since 1996, over eighty women have worked to create more than 3,000 Maya Dolls, weaving traditional clothing which resembles their own. They carefully sew and braid the hair and embroider the face. This has been a source of great pride for these Mayan women who live in remote highland villages of Guatemala as well as needed income," was the description under a picture of four Guatemalan women of varying ages, sitting under a tree in the lush green grass, creating beautiful dolls.

Obviously these women were Guatemala's poor. Could one of these doll-makers be Lucinda's grandmother? Aunt? Older sister? Mother? (If she lived her life in Guatemala, could it one day have been Lucinda?)

Antonia is the doll I chose to purchase. She has long, black, braided hair tied with red ribbons, charcoal-colored eyes, and a sweet smile on her coffee-colored face. Her blouse, called a *huipil*, is white with red and black decorative stitching and *quetzels* (Guatemalan blue birds) embroidered on it; women from the same villages would all wear the same *huipil*. Antonia's wrap-around skirt, called a *corte*, is beautifully woven with a myriad of rich, burgundy-colored threads. In Guatemala, girls between the ages of eight and twelve learn from their grandmothers and mothers how to weave; Antonia's dress is representative of that craftsmanship. The doll's clothing resembles the dress of the doll crafters in the Internet photograph. Hand made in Guatemala, this doll will be the first doll in Lucinda's collection. More importantly, it will be a tangible tie to her culture and to her homeland.

I want to do more to help those in need, especially those with a tie to Lucinda, but the adoption fees we are paying are so exorbitant that I am doing all that I can right now to make the world a better place. If Lucinda's birthmother had enough money, would she raise Lucinda herself? Or would she still believe that Lucinda's life would be better outside Guatemala with us? That I'll never know.

I have to have faith in God that what is to be, will be. And despite our many differences, I bet Lucinda's birthmother feels that way, too.

Chapter 26:

Listserv Links

The computer is an amazing machine. Hooked up to the Internet, with a couple of mouse clicks, my computer transports me into a whole new world. And in that cyber world there exists a group of amazing people from all different walks of life who come together on a daily basis to "chat," ask questions, and receive support from those who really are the only ones who truly understand the anguish of all this waiting. They are all members of the online Guatemalan Adoption listserv that I've come to know and love.

In the days before computerized information, I imagine that most people didn't really understand all the nooks and crannies of international adoption. When the agency director called, you got information. When you called the agency, you may or may not have received information about your pending case. All the information about Guatemala and adoption you learned through word of mouth or library research, if anything substantial existed. It was an "ignorance is bliss" time, I think, because what you didn't know most likely didn't hurt you. For example, if your case was kicked out of PGN, you didn't even know. All you knew was that your case was in the courts, and when it was released, you would get a call, "the call," from the adoption agency.

Nowadays, people can come together and share their experiences and knowledge like never before. The Internet provides Guatemalan adopting families a "living room" of sorts to sit and chat and share what we know and what we feel.

In the beginning, I was constantly online to read emails from members of the listserv in order to know everything I could know about adoption from Guatemala. It surprised me to learn that the baby could come home with black and blue-looking birthmarks called Mongolian Spots, and this shouldn't scare me, because this is common. I also learned that her vaccinations may have to be repeated when she comes home to the United States, because the vaccinations she gets in Guatemala may not be the right dosage or may not have been administered at all. I was surprised to hear that babies often slept with the foster mothers in a bed rather than a crib. Also, it was cultural to pierce a girl baby's earlobes, a symbol that she is loved. I read with interest a heated debate on gender: should adoptive families be able to choose a boy or a girl for their referral? And I learned all about the technical terminology and the specifics involved in the entire adoption process.

Is it good that I know so much?

I was able to find comfort and consolation from so many kind-hearted listserv members when I posted about Lucinda's birthmother's disappearance. Through networking on the list a woman passed along Manfred's name. I celebrated with those who got "the call" to bring home their babies, and I shared my sorrow with those who lost a referral. I discovered amazing information about children's books about adoption, Guatemalan charity organizations, various adoption agencies, state readoption procedures, INS red-tape cutting, and more! It's been quite an education.

However, at the same time, I heard all the "horror" stories of cases being "stuck" in the system, felt the anguish in the words of parents who lost children, who had to endure years of infertility or years of single hood, hoping and wishing for a child to call their own.

Every bump, every bad turn, every step backward our case took, I knew exactly what was going on, and sometimes that knowledge was too much to bear. And with every Guatemalan court ruling that rocked the adoption world, I was there to share the anxiety and uncertainty with others in the same proverbial boat.

Like so much in today's day, there is good and bad in everything. For all the sleepless nights worrying that I spent, pondering what others said on the listserv about their cases and seeing a possible link to mine, there were also those mornings when I was equipped with the knowledge to push our adoption agency a little harder for information and to get them to act faster. Knowledge is power, any way you look at it.

I've met amazing friends on the listserv, and for them I am extremely grateful. There's Karen who first answered my email when I requested feedback from those who had older sister-younger sister ten-year age gaps. She emailed me to tell me about her younger sister whom her family adopted from Asia when Karen was the same age as my Miranda. She told me about how excited she was, how thrilled she felt about being an older sister, how wonderful it was to share her life after so many years without a sibling. She reassured me that all would be fine, that it was a do-able situation.

From that point on, she and I exchanged emails, voicing our excitement and our frustrations with the adoption journey. After giving birth to three boys, she and her husband were adopting a baby girl. Her journey started a little before mine, so Karen was the "expert" that I followed during the twists and turns each step of the way that she experienced first. When she was feeling down, I suddenly was feeling strong, sending her "hang in there" emails, telling her all would be fine. And the same was true in reverse. Karen got "the call" at the beginning of summer, and I was so delighted to hear her good news! When she returned home from Guatemala with her seven month old daughter, she told me in detail all about her experience, knowing I wanted to know everything because I would hopefully be following in her footsteps soon.

And then there was Celeste who in a roundabout way got my name from someone on the listserv. Three years ago, Celeste and her husband, fellow New Jerseyans, adopted a baby girl from Guatemala. And Celeste's son is a few years older than Miranda. Immediately Celeste and I became friends, and her emails (and, now, phone calls) continue to be a source of inspiration. She tells me about her experiences adopting her daughter from Guatemala, gives me advice about transitions, family, and travel, and has become my cheerleader when setbacks occur. When I talk with Celeste, I know she really understands what I am feeling and thinking. She was once in my shoes. And with every laugh or sigh we share, I know I'm not alone. She is a good friend.

There are others who have opened up their hearts and stories to me, too many to mention by name, but each and every one has made this adoption journey an incredible experience for me. It has reaffirmed my faith that people are good, kind, generous, and caring. To know that hundreds of orphans will join these people's families and thrive in a bounty of love, who will learn tolerance, patience, and acceptance, and who will always know how much they are wanted, how much their parents struggled to bring them home—this makes me feel good, more hopeful about humanity. I am grateful for the technology that has brought us all together.

Chapter 27:

To Lucinda Rubi On Her First Birthday

Dear Lucinda,

Here at home the yellow, orange, and red leaves are clinging to the tree branches. A slight breeze of autumn wind plucks them from the trees and they gracefully twirl to the ground.

The air is getting colder. In the mornings, you can see your breath. But in the afternoons, the sun shines, and if you close your eyes and hold your face up toward the sky, you feel the warmth on your eyelids and across the bridge of your nose.

It's sweater season again, and in a couple of months we'll have to don the heavy winter coats before we head outdoors. We have a smiling orange pumpkin decorating our front door, and on the post on the porch, a green-faced witch hangs to greet trick-or-treaters on the 31st. Your sister Miranda is going to be dressed as a devil; she was hoping you would be an angel for your first venture out into the neighborhood to collect candy, but since you are still not yet home, she will be a solo devil awaiting her angel in Guatemala. Don't worry—she has grand plans for you for other Halloweens to come! It's an American tradition that I know you will love.

Your bedroom is now painted and polished and ready for you. The mint-green walls will soothe you when you first open your eyes in the morning. The sun streaks in through the blinds, and you will have a big smile on your face when you wake up and see the new day beginning around you.

The shelves are filled with books; some are Miranda's favorites when she was your age, and some are brand new because I just couldn't resist. What you need to know about Mommy is that she LOVES books. So don't worry that we haven't had a chance to glimpse together *Goodnight, Moon* or *I'll*

Love You Forever or all of those funny Dr. Seuss stories—we'll tackle them with vigor when you are home and we cuddle together on the rocking chair.

English won't be familiar to you at first, but you will see how fast it will become second nature to your lips! I will teach you. Something tells me that when you look into my eyes and I look into yours, we will understand each other; no words will be needed right away…

The drawers and shelves in your bureau and closet are bare. I have been so tempted to buy all those pretty little dresses, overalls, bathing suits, snow suits… Each season brings new versions of pink outfits that dance before my eyes. Miranda and I always take the opportunity to walk through baby departments in stores, touching the little clothes. We talk about which outfit we WOULD buy for you if we knew you were coming home today. Then we get quiet when we realize that you're not here…but we squeeze our hands together and walk away, determined that ONE DAY SOON all THREE of us girls will go shopping to fill up that closet of yours! You won't even be home one week and all of your clothes will be neatly folded and ready for wear. The relatives are anxious to send you crocheted sweaters and hats and booties. So don't worry—as soon as I know you're coming home, I am going to go shopping with Miranda and buy lots of clothes in your size! You will be quite fashionable.

Stuffed animals, dolls, and toys are awaiting your arrival. I bet you will be ready to play when you get home! Here in the United States there are toys that make sounds, that wind up, that pop up, that vibrate, that sing, that dance, that move… My favorites are the old-fashioned ones, though, the ones that you can quietly, on your own timetable, touch, hug, throw, and imagine in lots of magical ways. Miranda saved some of hers for you, and when you are ready, I'm going to put you in a shopping cart and we'll take a trip to Toys R Us to buy some other ones! You won't believe your eyes when we walk down the aisles and you see so many colors, shapes, and sizes! It's a day that I am looking forward to.

Daddy, Miranda, and I bought a carriage for you. We'll have fun taking walks and admiring the trees and the flowers and the outdoor cats that sometimes cross our paths. Miranda likes to test out the umbrella stroller that we purchased in the beginning of summer. It has little brown teddy bears in sailor suits and pictures of boats on the fabric. Miranda likes to pretend that you're already home, and she walks you (you being substituted for a baby doll) in the playroom basement. The wheels are pristine white, but when you come home, they'll see some ware and mileage, that's for sure! That's how it's meant to be, so I won't mind if it doesn't look brand new anymore. It's yours.

Our cats Ed and Ashley aren't yet sure what all the fuss is about. They enjoyed watching us paint your bedroom walls, and they like jumping up on the changing table. Once we heard a jingle coming from your room, and when I went in to investigate, I saw one of the cats playing with a rattle that I bought for you when you were born! A butterfly is inside the circle, and it has a big smiling grin on its friendly face! That waits for you, too, even if you may be a little too old to like shaking a rattle. You might find it amusing. I know that the cats will amuse you! They are funny to watch, and most of the time, if you pet their soft fur, they will start to purr and sit near you. You will like that.

Today is Thursday, October 23, 2003, your first birthday, my Lucy, and even though you are in Guatemala still and we are way over here in the United States, we are still a family. Today we will bake a cake, light candles, and celebrate your first birthday in the world! It's sad, thinking about what we haven't been able to do together in your first year, but what makes us happy is thinking about all the times together we have ahead of us.

You have a daddy that made sure not a single speck of green paint ended up on your white ceiling…a big sister who carries to school every day your picture in her wallet…grandparents in New Hampshire and Florida who smile at your pictures on their refrigerators… and a mommy who thinks about you when she wakes up, who wonders what you are doing throughout the day, and prays to God to take care of you each night. The love, the family, the furniture, the toys, the books, the cats—they're all here, waiting for you when you come home.

Tonight, when you close your eyes to go to sleep, I hope you feel a gentle breeze graze your soft cheek as God whispers in your ear "Happy Birthday, Lucinda! You are so loved!" Then *my* birthday wish on your birthday will come true… Happy 1st Birthday, my sweet Lucinda!

Love,
Mommy

Chapter 28:

Adoption-Speak

Unless you or someone you know has adopted a child, you may not be familiar with the "lingo" associated with adoption. I didn't know the proper way to label the woman who gave birth to the child we are adopting, for instance, when we first started our adoption journey. Calling her Lucinda's mother wasn't right; after all, *I* was going to be her mother. Miranda at first called her Lucinda's "real" mother, but that didn't sit right with us, either. Was she more real than I am? We started to think about definitions of very common words that have lots of emotional meaning. Who is a mother? Who is a father? And who is the one who selflessly gives a child up for adoption?

I learned from word of mouth, the most current books, and our social worker with whom we met last summer that there are specific words to use when discussing key people in adoption situations. For instance, the woman who gave birth to Lucinda is Lucinda's birthmother. I, on the other hand, am Lucinda's mother. Since those of us who adopt love our children as much if not more than if they were our very own biological offspring, there is no need to call mothers like me "adoptive mothers." Being a mother regardless of the way it evolves deserves the full title with a capital M!

That also goes for everyone else in the family. It's a no-no to say, "This is Lucinda's adopted family" when referring to us. We are her family. Period. Whatever would be said to Miranda regarding her relationship to us is equal to what should be said to Lucinda regarding her relationship to us. There is no difference, nor should any distinction be made about how each came to be loved by us.

Now does that mean the adoption is ignored? No. Not at all. Lucinda will have a life book that I am making for her that chronicles all of her pictures and all the adoption updates and all the feelings we had waiting for her to come home to us. In the adoption world, a life book is essentially the story of the child from referral to present. Most children have a baby book that chronicles all the "firsts;" this life book is similar. But, like in Lucinda's case, we don't know when her very first tooth made its debut, and we don't know the exact day she learned to sit up independently or even what foods she likes or dislikes. There are lots of unknowns when it comes to adoption. If possible, the foster mother or the orphanage fills in those blanks. But if not, then they do not receive blank marks in the baby book. What is celebrated is what is known and what was anticipated during the time you were apart. It gives the child a sense of identity and an acknowledgment about how much he or she was wanted and loved.

What do you do when your child is asked to do a family tree project for school? The first thing to do is talk with the teacher. It's important for educators to realize that not all children know their exact roots. Instead, doing a family circles project includes those who may be adopted without singling them out. Rather than drawing a tree with many branches, one assembles circles to show how each person in a family is related. If all the children do this project instead of the family tree project, everyone is happy and no one's feelings are hurt. So educating the educators at school is important for those who adopt.

Lastly, there's a day called Gotcha Day that people in adoption circles use to refer to the day they officially became a complete family when the adoption concludes and the child is finally home. Some in the adoption world don't like that term. Others adore it. Personally, I think Gotcha Day for me was the day Lucinda jumped into my heart. It was the day I first saw her picture and realized, "Yes, that's my baby girl!" Those who celebrate Gotcha Day celebrate it as if it were a birthday or anniversary. It is, after all, a very important day to the family and to the child. It shows the child how important he or she is in the family. Just as one would celebrate a birthday when a child is born, one acknowledges with fanfare the day everyone came together through adoption.

I've heard funny instances where biological brothers and sisters get jealous that they don't have a Gotcha Day celebration. It's not unusual, in these families, to have a Gotcha Day to not only celebrate the day of a finalized adoption but also the day the biological child came home from the hospital and joined the family! Or other families bypass Gotcha Day for Family Day, the day when the family united. Either way, it's a celebration and a time to reflect on how important everyone is in the family no matter how they became exclusive members.

Will people come up to us and/or to Lucinda and ask about her adoption? Most likely, since I hear that from others. What am I supposed to say when nosy people ask, "How much did you pay for her?" and "Why did her mother give her up?" These are typical questions that well-meaning people say when they don't understand adoption etiquette. Some in the adoption world say to be up front and direct, explaining how those questions are offensive and hurtful. Others say to be evasive or to make a joke to side-step the questions. Others say to be honest. It's important for those who are ignorant about adoption to be educated. But it's also important for people to show respect and think twice before asking personal questions.

The world of adoption is complicated and, at the same time, very simple when you think about it. Love is Love is Love. It doesn't really matter the circumstances. So the next time you see a family with children who may not look the same as the parents, remember how special it is that in this great big world, people know no boundaries when it comes to love and family. Moms are moms, Dads are dads, and siblings love to tease and play with each other no matter how the family was created.

Consider yourself educated!

Chapter 29:

An Emotional Basket Case!

It's October, and we're still waiting for our adoption to finalize in Guatemala. I've experienced every emotion along the way:

Nervousness: is foreign adoption right for us?

Euphoria: receiving Lucinda's picture last November 7th and thinking, "There she is! She's the one!"

Excitement: the adoption paperwork is finally making its way to Guatemala; the process begins.

Joy: receiving monthly pictures of our Lucinda and daydreaming about her.

Indecisiveness: should we start planning for a spring arrival? Maybe we shouldn't buy too many things…just in case…you never know…

Fear: Lucinda's birthmother is missing; our adoption is jeopardized and derailed.

Panic: If Lucinda's birthmother doesn't return, will we forever lose Lucinda? What will happen to her?

Frustration: If Lucinda's birthmother already signed away her parental rights, stating her desire to have her child adopted by a family in the United States, why can't we go forward and adopt Lucinda?

Heartbreak: After waiting several months to see if Lucinda's birthmother would surface, we are told to move on and accept a new referral.

Mourning: Saying goodbye to Lucinda in our hearts, we shed many tears.

Hopeful: We prepare to accept a new referral. We pray this adoption will be successful.

Numb: The adoption laws in Guatemala are changing, and we cannot register our new referral; we begin to accept the fact that most likely this is the end of the adoption road for us.

Disbelief: Lucinda's birthmother returns! We move forward with Lucinda!

Cautious Optimism: Will Lucinda's birthmother keep her court appointment in Guatemala and sign the necessary paperwork so the adoption can continue?

Thrilled: Lucinda's adoption is back on track and we're making progress in the Guatemalan court system. Hallelujah!

Upset: Over the summer, adoptions are at a virtual standstill while the Hague Treaty is debated and eventually defeated by Guatemala's Supreme Court.

Jealousy: Other cases are receiving PGN approval. I am so jealous when I see others elated to be bringing home children even younger than Lucinda. When will it be our turn?

Anger: Why is our file gathering dust in PGN? When will they release the case so we can bring home Lucinda?

What do I currently feel? Pessimism. I feel pessimistic and deflated right now, in all honesty. I have hoped and prayed for a positive outcome for so many months, that now, virtually at the end, I am tired and discouraged. I am not ready to totally throw in the towel, but at the same time, I am preparing myself, mentally, that maybe, just maybe, Lucinda will never come home to us. Maybe something else will stand in the way: a new law or treaty, a new requirement... I desperately want to believe the best, but I am bracing myself for the worst.

These days, when I return home after being out of the house, I immediately look at the caller ID to see if anyone from the adoption agency has called. It could be any time now... But that "any time now" has been stretching longer and longer and longer. My mother says that when I least expect it, the call will come, but how can that be when I have been expecting it for months now? Our paperwork just needs a signature. And that's what we've been waiting all these months for...for one person's name scribbled across a document that will finalize Lucinda's fate.

As my Nanny used to say, "A watched pot never boils." So I am keeping busy, being productive and useful, keeping that smile on my face. But inevitably someone asks, "Any news about Lucinda?" and my face just drains of all its blood and, pale, my eyes instantly glossy, I fumble an excuse and end with "so we're still waiting." Of course, I don't blame others for asking. It's not polite if they ignore the situation, but I do kick myself over and over again these days wishing that I kept the adoption a grand secret to be revealed only when people saw me out and about with a baby girl wrapped in my arms.

"Good things come to those who wait," my mother keeps telling me. Fantastic things must be coming around the corner, after all this waiting time! Sigh… There's always tomorrow. Now I really know what living for today really means.

Chapter 30:

FINALLY GREAT NEWS!!!

On Thursday, October 30th, I received new pictures of our Lucinda. As always, my heart beat a little faster as I double clicked to see photos of my baby girl. I smiled, seeing her standing for the first time, wearing denim overalls, an orange turtleneck, white lacy socks, and her shiny little black Mary-Jane shoes. Her curly hair was in pigtails, the orange bows matching her outfit. I was smitten, as always! In another photo, I saw Lucy smiling, her mouth open just enough for me to see two top teeth! Oh, our girl was getting older, developing nicely, resembling more and more a curious, sweet toddler.

I was so happy to see her growth, her development, her smile, and just knowing she was well cared for and thriving gave me great comfort. But did I want to hold that little girl in my arms, kiss those soft, chubby cheeks, peer into those black-olive eyes and say for the first time, "Hello, sweetie! I am your mommy! And I love you so much!" Bittersweet it always is on picture day...

I told myself that just for today I was glad to get the pictures. Long ago when we first started the adoption journey, I told myself that I would be satisfied if just one thing, no matter how big or small, occurred each week, moving our case forward. So that was the one thing that God sent my way for the week, I figured, and I was happy to have that.

I forwarded the pictures online to Dave and some friends and relatives; anticipating their obvious question, "When do you think Lucy will come home?", I wrote, "It's taking a very long time, but we're still waiting, hoping, and praying that Lucinda will be home soon."

Then I went about my day. I learned throughout this journey that I needed to immediately move forward, not look back, and not wallow in the sadness or the frustration that accompanies a long wait for something wonderful just out of reach.

When Miranda came home from school, she saw the new pictures of her little sister, and she was delighted to see her standing. Since Lucy was standing, maybe even walking, Miranda was most concerned that her little sister wouldn't want to be carried. This, of course, is what Miranda really wants: to carry her little sister in her arms everywhere and all the time! I reassured her that Lucy, though now one, was still considered a baby, and that she would love being held long after she was too big to be hoisted on a hip. Satisfied, Miranda smiled; she learned to move on, too.

That evening, while Miranda got her red devil costume ready for Halloween the next day and Dave watched the news on TV, I tutored students online at Tutor.com. (It's hard to keep a teacher who loves to teach away from students!) Around 7 p.m. my computer's alarm bell rang, signaling me that an email from Manfred just arrived. In between students, I had time to read his email right away.

As soon as I saw smiley faces on the subject line, I knew this was going to make me happy. Earlier in the day I sent Manfred and Edwin the new photos of Lucinda that I received from the adoption agency, and I figured they were writing to say she was beautiful.

But it was even better than that! I read the following email:

"Good evening, Amy. Sorry for the delay in getting back to you .... but certain information we just have to re-check and confirm twice before telling ....My dearest Amy & David, it is our most fond and sincere pleasure to inform you that you've got PGN approval !!!!!!! Your file is in the submission / retrieval office, ready to be retrieved! Amy & David .... let me just hug you !!! Know what the funniest thing was .... I received the photo of Lucinda ... AND JUST KNEW IT SHOULD HAPPEN TODAY !!!!! All our love, dear Amy and David !" Manfred.

As soon as I saw the words 'PGN APPROVAL' I screamed—yes, I *literally* screamed!

Dave and Miranda came rushing down the stairs, asking me what was wrong, and I shouted, *"WE'RE OUT OF PGN!!!"*

Tears immediately welled up in Dave's eyes while Miranda jumped up and down, shouting and laughing! I stood up from the computer and wrapped my arms around Dave's neck, and then the three of us did a family hug. We were at a loss for words, but we were just so incredibly thankful and HAPPY that we knew *for sure* that we were indeed going to have our Lucy home. She would be ours. Dave and I would be her parents, Miranda would be her big sister, and she would live with us and be a part of our family. Lucinda was about to start a new life in a new country with her forever family.

I went straight for the phone.

Dialing my parents' number in Florida, I had a gigantic smile on my face, and I felt dizzy, as if something big and strong had just hit me over the head. As soon as I heard my mother's voice, I blurted out, "We're out of PGN!!!" However, there was dead silence on the other end of the phone. That I wasn't expecting. So I said, a little calmer this time so my words could be heard, "Mom, it's me, Amy! We finally got out of PGN! Lucy is coming home!" and no sooner had I stopped talking then my mother started screaming, cheering, thanking God, yelling the news to my father in the next room…

It reminded me of the same telephone call I made eleven years ago, when I was in West Virginia, in the hospital, calling my parents just after the birth of Miranda. When I told my mom that I had the baby and it was a girl, she reacted the exact same way, almost verbatim! And my dad reacted the same way, too. More reserved, he took the phone receiver (and I could still hear my mother shouting with excitement in the background), and asked me to tell him the details. I could tell he was smiling, hearing the news.

He said, "Whenever you need your mother to come, she will be there. I can get her to you as soon as possible." I had to laugh. My father thinks that my mother is the only expert on the planet when it comes to caring for babies, and despite the fact that Miranda is eleven and Dave and I seemed to have done quite well on our own all these years, the offering of my mother to fly out as soon as I needed her was his way of giving me the very best he had to offer. Despite the fact that my mother is annoyed when he "offers" her, I told her that she should feel honored that he thinks so highly of her maternal skills. Naturally, when she returned to the phone, now a bit more composed, she offered to come out as soon as I needed her, this time giving me her own offer.

It is a call like this that makes you feel so happy and so fortunate and special to have parents who really unconditionally love you and delight in your happiness.

The next call went to Dave's parents. When I got on the phone with my mother-in-law, she was elated, ecstatic, laughing, happy! I relayed to her the details of the news, since Dave is more matter-of-fact, and she was just overjoyed to hear Lucinda was going to be home soon. She, too, offered to come out and help us.

In fact, everyone we called, friends and family members, near and far, offered to help us in any way that they could. Their arms were wide open to welcome home our newest family member, long awaited, and already very much loved.

That night as I got into bed, the new pictures of Lucinda next to me on the night table, I told Dave that I was afraid to go to sleep, afraid that all of this happiness would disappear. I had been wishing for this news for so, so, so long, but what if it was just a dream? I couldn't stop smiling. I couldn't stop saying, "She's finally going to be coming home! She's finally going to be living with us! She's finally going to have her family!" I didn't want to lose this incredible high.

Eventually I did conk out and fall asleep, most likely from sheer exhaustion, but when I awoke, it was 1 a.m. Even in the darkness, I couldn't help smiling. I remembered! But I had to be sure.

I tiptoed downstairs and flicked on the light in the kitchen. Adjusting my eyes, I stood over the email from Manfred (that I printed) and read it again…and again…and again! It was real.

And I thanked God, aloud, for making my dream come true and answering all those prayers I've uttered to Him throughout the adoption…

God is Good! Life is Good! And I don't think I'm ever coming down from Cloud Nine!

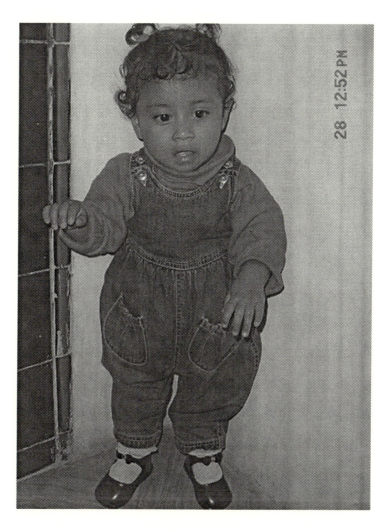

This is our final photo of Lucinda sent to us via computer from the adoption agency. Lucy is 12 months of age and it is the first time we see her standing! We study this picture over and over and over again. Several hours after receiving this photo we learn from Manfred that we have exited PGN and Lucy is coming home soon!

Chapter 31:

Miranda Is Charmed…

Last year when Miranda turned ten, we bought her a charm bracelet with an adorable teddy bear charm, a light green peridot birthstone in its belly. We told Miranda that now that she was in the "double digits" as she so fondly reminded us over and over again as nine became ten, we thought she was now old enough to appreciate a very special gift of jewelry, a bracelet that would symbolize all the significant events in her life. Thrilled at being considered "old enough" for *anything*, Miranda loved the bracelet and proudly wore it.

That year Miranda developed a love of music. After enjoying the recorder in third grade band, she "graduated" to the flute. But Miranda didn't take to the flute, and eventually, she decided it wasn't her destiny.

However, she decided the piano was. Often experimenting on her electronic keyboard at home, Miranda would play songs by ear. She asked to take lessons so she could learn how to read music and play "real" songs. During the summer between fifth and sixth grade, Miranda devoted thirty minutes a week to piano lessons and several hours a week to practice. That summer Miranda fell in love with her keyboard and quickly excelled, learning to read music notes and play songs using sheet music. When we visited her great grandfather in the nursing home in the fall, Miranda played the piano in the social room, delighting my grandparents and parents who marveled at the family's new virtuoso!

Not surprisingly, the next charm on her charm bracelet was a silver music note symbolizing her passion for music.

"I want my next charm to represent my sister," said Miranda matter-of-factly during the adoption. She had her eye on a few charms that represented babies, and she wanted to get that charm on the bracelet to "cement" the idea that indeed she was going to be an older sister, that indeed a baby girl from Guatemala with whom we fell in love through pictures was indeed coming home to live with us forever.

Hesitant, I asked Miranda to wait until we got the final good news, that Lucinda was indeed a legal member of our family and that she was imminently coming home to us. Typical of a preteen, Miranda complained, but she accepted my reluctance and didn't push.

When we finally received the long-awaited news that our case was out of PGN and Lucinda would be coming home in just a few weeks, Miranda burst into cheers, and reminded me, very quickly, that it was time to get that charm! So off we went to the mall a few days later, determined to find the perfect charm to represent Miranda's becoming a sister.

Through the glass case at the jewelry store, we eyed the baby charms: storks, baby shoes, teddy bears, angels… It was going to be a hard decision to make. Miranda asked the sales clerk if she could see up close the baby carriage charm, and she was intrigued when she saw that the wheels actually turned! But, for some reason, she hesitated, saying she wanted to look more. So we did just that, wandering from one store to another, looking at the charms and trying to determine which would be the perfect fit.

Miranda saw it first. On the turnstile of charms representing every life event, Miranda pointed at a gold heart: one half said "big sister" and the other half said "little sister." Beautiful roses decorated each side. It was the kind of charm that could be separated so both sisters could each have a piece of the heart.

Holding it delicately in her hand, Miranda said, "Mom, if I get this one, I can give Lucy the other half of the charm when she's ten and gets her own charm bracelet!" I smiled, touched by the tenderness and sentimentality of my oldest. She reasoned that the carriage and the stork charms were not as special as the sister charm, because one day she may be a mom, but this is the only time she'd be a sister. I agreed with her logical thinking, and we purchased the heart charm. Miranda kept looking at it in its velvet case all the way home.

Over the weekend Dave and I put the finishing touches on Lucinda's bedroom. The crib is up, and the room is ready. Miranda is busy practicing putting the bar of the crib up and down, because she is determined to be the first person Lucinda sees in the morning to greet her as she starts the day.

And on Miranda's wrist sits the newest charm on her charm bracelet, promising her that this is real, that she truly is a big sister. And she is ready to meet her already much loved younger sibling who, in nine years, will add a golden half charm to her charm bracelet, compliments of her big sister.

Chapter 32: Dear Lucinda, You're Coming Home!

Letter from Miranda to Lucinda recorded in Miranda's journal

11/16/03

Dear Lucinda,

I have been waiting so long and have been so patient! Now I cannot think about anything other than your coming home! Mom and Dad should be going to Guatemala on the 23rd (next Sunday). I am staying with my friend until Tuesday. On Tuesday I will stay with Grandma and Grandpa. On Wednesday, at 5 p.m., we will all go to the airport to pick you up!

I hope you like me!

Just for Wednesday, I think I will sleep with you on the cot and spend as much time with you as possible. I hate looking in your room now, because it is empty. The clock doesn't make me feel any better, because time goes too slow to watch. I wish I had a fairy godparent so I could wish it were Wednesday right now. That is impossible, but it might happen.

I know now you don't know who I am, but you will soon. I also know you won't come running to hug me like I'd hoped, but I understand.

Do not stop believing! Lucinda Rubi Jean, the Shore-Jean family is coming! I love you!

Love,
Miranda Jean
Your brand new big sister!

Chapter 33:

Another Blip on the Adoption Radar Screen

Typically when a case exits PGN, it takes a minimum of ten days and a maximum of three weeks to get the necessary documents (the child's new birth certificate and Guatemalan passport are issued and new documents are translated from Spanish to English) into the U.S. Embassy in Guatemala City for approval. A "pink slip" is issued within forty-eight hours, the child sees an embassy doctor for a last physical, and then the adopting parents go to the embassy with their child to submit final documents, pay more money, and get the stamp of approval, finalizing the adoption and allowing the family to bring the child back with them to the United States.

That's how it is supposed to work… But of course, in our rocky thirteen-month journey, there had to be a hitch.

Our adoption agency couldn't get our Guatemalan attorney to work fast enough to get the necessary documents gathered, certified, and submitted to the U.S. Embassy. We heard lots of excuses, but in the end, we, again, were powerless to act and had to just wait and see.

With Thanksgiving coming, the embassy would be closed in observance of the holiday, and appointments are never scheduled on Fridays. So it was imperative for us to get our paperwork submitted to the embassy by Monday, November 17, 2003. That way we'd be issued a pink slip on Wednesday, Lucy could have her doctor's appointment on Thursday or Friday, and we'd be able to go to the embassy with her on Monday or Tuesday to finalize her adoption and bring her home Wednesday, the night before Thanksgiving.

That's how it should have been. However, that's not what happened.

We paid extra money to the adoption agency so the facilitator in Guatemala could hire a courier and expedite Lucinda's new birth certificate. That was one hundred dollars. Then, in addition to the two hundred dollars we paid for new translations of documents, we paid an additional fifty-eight dollars to expedite the translations so they would be ready and on the attorney's desk in Guatemala City on Monday morning, November 17th.

And they were. But the attorney didn't sign them, infuriating everyone behind the scenes who were desperately trying to get this done so Lucy could celebrate her first Thanksgiving at home with her family.

On Tuesday the papers were certified and signed, but the attorney didn't get them submitted to the Embassy; he thought the line was too long. When he saw twenty-one people ahead of him at the embassy window, he turned around and headed back to his office.

What's another day? Well, nothing if you don't celebrate Thanksgiving. But to us, it meant everything.

That meant that our pink slip would not be issued until at least Monday, November 24th, the day after my husband and I were scheduled to travel to Guatemala. It would be risky. What if the pink slip wasn't issued on Monday? What if we couldn't get Lucy in for a doctor's appointment before Wednesday? What if the embassy closed for Thanksgiving before we finished and we were "stuck" in Guatemala, not able to return on our flight that we scheduled?

What about my parents who were flying to New Jersey from Florida to spend Thanksgiving with us and to meet their much-awaited little granddaughter? What about eleven-year old Miranda who was nervous about her parents flying out of the country without her? If we didn't come home when we were supposed to, we'd have to make long-distance arrangements for Miranda when my parents had to leave!

We just couldn't take these risks.

So at 7 p.m. on Thursday, November 20th, I was on the phone with my parents, seeing if they could extend their travel plans to accommodate our new travel plans the following week to Guatemala. That way Miranda could stay with them at our home and go to school without too much disruption during our absence. When I hung up the phone with them, I called our travel agent and altered our airline tickets to accommodate the new plans. (Luckily we spent the extra two hundred dollars per ticket in order to make changes without penalty. Somehow we just knew that the end of the adoption couldn't be any smoother than the rest of the experience had been!)

Here were the original plans that I made for travel before Thanksgiving:

We leave Sunday, November 23rd.

Miranda packs her suitcase and stays with her friend from Sunday through Tuesday (all school days are half days the week of Thanksgiving, making the upheaval on Miranda easier.)

On Tuesday, November 25th, my parents arrive from Florida and an airport limousine service drives them to our home.

That evening, Miranda's friend's mother drives Miranda with her suitcase back to our house so she can stay with my parents.

Wednesday, November 26th, Miranda and my parents drive to Newark's Liberty Airport and await our plane due to land at approximately 6 p.m.

Lucinda's home! We're home! And we celebrate Thanksgiving the next day.

Here were the "requests" I made to our Adoption Agency after those plans were ruined:

We would travel to Guatemala instead on Saturday, November 29th (because we couldn't get any flights on Sunday, one of the heaviest travel days of the year.)

On Sunday morning, we would finally meet Lucinda at the hotel. (The agency doesn't typically unite children and parents on a Saturday or a Sunday, but after a very long adoption wait and having to deal with the incompetence of our Guatemalan lawyer, we were now demanding to be the exception to the rule.)

Monday, December 1st we would go to the embassy, pink slip and medical report in hand, and finalize the adoption.

We would return to New Jersey on Tuesday or Wednesday (just in case…)

That night, after realizing that we had now an additional week of waiting for Lucinda, we were very disappointed. We had come so far, and we had yet one more delay. Miranda cried, big tears falling from her eyes. She was upset that she would not be able to play with her sister during her time off from school for the Thanksgiving holiday. Always wanting to follow the rules, Miranda did not want to miss school days, and Lucinda would be coming home in the middle of a school week. I tried to comfort her and her disappointment.

Dave fumed, furious that what should have happened, didn't. Presentations and meetings at work that were meticulously rescheduled to clear his calendar were now sitting on the new dates we would be in Guatemala. I reminded him that when I went into labor with Miranda, I was seven days past my due date, and he had to juggle things at work back then to accommodate Mother Nature and our family. Everything could be fixed.

And I was once again feeling numb and telling myself to remember it was just a delay. We had been through worse.

The next morning was a new day! Yet the clouds quickly rolled in…

I received an email from the U.S. Embassy in Guatemala City, telling me that our visas were cleared for travel, but our FBI fingerprinting cards on record were going to expire on November 25th, 2003.

Fifteen months earlier, on a sunny, humid day in August, with so much hope and optimism in our hearts, we waited in a long, Newark, New Jersey line to get fingerprinted, one of the very first steps in foreign adoption. And just days shy of our newly-planned departure to Guatemala to finally meet and bring home our precious little girl, our expired fingerprints would prohibit us from leaving the Land of Eternal Spring in Central America with our baby.

I was on the phone, frantically talking with a representative at Newark's INS, who scheduled a new fingerprinting appointment for us the next morning at 8 a.m. Dave would not be happy—another workday spoiled. But it was necessary. Our fingerprints had to clear and we had to get written approval before we could travel to bring home Lucy. And Thanksgiving was going to lessen our fingerprint-processing time. Another one hundred dollars we would spend to prove to our country that we were not arrested during the past fifteen months we've been trying to adopt.

Sigh……………

I just hope God realizes that we've finally hit our frustration limit! I truly believe that God never gives anyone more than he or she can handle, but I'm starting to question this last blip on the adoption radar screen!

Chapter 34:

The Thanksgiving Miracle

On the heaviest travel day of the year, the day before Thanksgiving, I was at home. Yet I traveled around the country and around the world by phone and by email, and it was one exhausting journey.

First, the background…

On Tuesday, I called Jocasta at INS who gave me the good news that the FBI cleared our new fingerprints. Since Dave and I had no arrests—not even a parking ticket between us, I was pretty confident that this would be the outcome, but with our luck, I held my breath until I heard the good news. Dave traveled to Newark to pick up this covetous fingerprinting document that we needed to bring with us to Guatemala. All day long I was on the telephone with our adoption agency, trying to find out if the U.S. Embassy in Guatemala issued to us the "pink slip", giving us the "all clear" sign to travel and bring home our beautiful Lucinda.

By the end of the day, we still had not received word, and that worried me.

Wednesday, the last day government offices would be open before the Thanksgiving holiday weekend, I kissed Miranda in the morning before she boarded her school bus and then immediately headed downstairs to check my email. I expected to hear from either the adoption agency or the U.S. Embassy in Guatemala, finally confirming that, yes, we did have that covetous pink slip. Typically forty-eight hours after the attorney submits the paperwork to the embassy, the pink slip is issued. (Note the word 'typically.')

In our case, this was not to be. My heart sank as I opened an email from the U.S. Embassy in Guatemala informing me that, no, the pink slip was not issued, because the Department of Homeland Security did not clear us. Now how could that be? No arrests…no speeding tickets or parking citations…no history of terrorist activity… How could Dave and I not clear homeland security?

Immediately I was on the telephone, calling our adoption agency. No answer. I left a frantic message. Then I dialed the U.S. Embassy in Guatemala. After pressing the number seven for English instructions, I was startled to hear the first option: if you have been arrested or are reporting a death of an American in Guatemala, press one… Oh boy! I waited patiently for the "you were denied a pink slip and don't know why, press twenty-five," but that option never presented itself. Instead, I was transferred to an operator who then transferred me to the adoption unit office and then I was greeted by a friendly voice on an answering machine telling me to email the office or leave a message; they don't accept phone calls.

Dead end.

Next, I called Dave at work, frantic. He calmed me down, telling me there had to be a reasonable explanation, telling me to contact Manfred for help. I hung up the phone and jumped on the computer, sending an S.O.S. email to my Guatemalan attorney-friend. Promptly, all the way from Guatemala City in a blink of an eye, I received an immediate response: he supplied me with phone numbers to contacts at the Embassy in Guatemala and the all-important telephone number in Guatemala City for our attorney who works with our adoption agency, the one who would REALLY be able to shed some light on this pink slip dilemma. The agency did not allow clients and attorneys to speak directly with each other. But I was about to break that rule.

Manfred also offered me one piece of advice: if all else fails, contact your U.S. Senator.

Fast forward the international telephone calls…the conversation with a woman who answered the phone at the attorney's office who was unable to speak English…the dead ends with the contacts at the Embassy who also have friendly answering machines…and let's go straight to the Senator's Office.

As a last ditch effort, with my heart beating wildly and my mind racing, I called New Jersey's Senator Frank Lautenberg in Washington, D.C. After explaining to the lady who picked up the phone that I needed help with an adoption case in Guatemala, I was given the Newark telephone number of Senator Lautenberg's office where I would find help on the day before government offices were scheduled to shut down for the long holiday weekend.

On the second ring, a friendly voice answered, and it wasn't a machine!

My call was immediately passed along to an attorney in charge of constituent concerns to whom I pleaded my case. By now it was 10 a.m. Telling me that Guatemala was experiencing turmoil with their adoption program which was causing the U.S. Embassy to have problems processing paperwork, this gentleman, Mr. John Bang, said he would do his best to try and uncover the problem. I faxed him pertinent information about our case (file numbers…baby's name…birth date…emails…) and then waited. And waited.

And waited.

By 4:30 that afternoon, I telephoned Mr. Bang to get an update. After all, it was the end of a workday before the beginning of a holiday, and I wanted to formally end the day with a run-down of events. He said, "I'm sorry I couldn't pull off a holiday miracle, but you will find email correspondence addressed to you that trace the steps I took today on your behalf. Perhaps you could email the gentleman at the U.S. Embassy in Guatemala with whom I spoke, telling him you'll literally be knocking on his door in Guatemala City on Monday morning."

I thanked Mr. Bang for his efforts, and with a heavy heart, headed to the computer to send another email.

That's when God stepped in…

I logged onto the computer and clicked on the most recent email from Guatemala City. It was addressed to Mr. Bang, copied to me, and it stated that our pink slip was issued at 3:45 p.m. Guatemala time.

I cried!

I printed the email for my records and followed the paper trail. Mr. Bang sent several emails to Guatemala on my behalf, all afternoon, tenaciously monitoring the situation, trying to uncover the reason why we weren't issued the pink slip. And his efforts did pay off in the form of victory!

At 4:45 p.m. I dashed off an email to Mr. Bang. I thanked him profusely, exclaiming, "You *did* pull off the holiday miracle!" I got offline, telephoned Dave and the adoption agency with the fantastic news, then headed back online to inform Manfred.

Surprisingly, I discovered I had a new email from Mr. Bang. He wrote: "Just when you give up hope, miracles happen. I am so happy you will have a happy holiday tomorrow. Please send me a picture of your completed family when you return from your trip!" My heart just swelled with happiness when I realized that this stranger in Newark in my Senator's office with whom by chance I crossed paths on the day before Thanksgiving just untangled the last international knot and completed our adoption! With no one left to battle, it was finally time to rejoice.

We were going to Guatemala in three days, and Lucy was finally, finally coming home!

Chapter 35:

Buying Diapers and Bracelets

Over the weekend, in addition to purchasing our Thanksgiving turkey, I also purchased two jumbo sized packages of diapers. What an amazing adrenaline rush, buying diapers! It finally signals that Lucinda is coming home. It is imminent! Over the past several months in my darkest hours I used to daydream about the days prior to traveling, how busy I'd be getting organized, buying clothes and diapers once I got Lucy's most current measurements from the adoption agency. I imagined the excitement of packing to travel to Guatemala and seeing my baby for the very first time. And now it was happening. Good things do come to those who wait, and we sure paid our dues waiting!

It is amazing how up and down life can be. Last night I was finally writing in Lucinda's baby book. It was time to make things permanent in ink. Her name...her family...her birth measurements... I arranged all of Lucy's pictures that we received over the past thirteen months, and I enjoyed flipping through the pages, numerous times, to see how our little Lucy grew from infancy to early toddlerhood. I reread my emails to friends and family and experienced again the bittersweet feelings that flooded my heart this past year. I added poems that were poignant, drawings that Miranda made showing her and her little sister hand-in-hand, official documents in Spanish that we received by fax... When she gets older and glances through her baby book, Lucy surely will know how much she was wanted and how much she was loved even before our eyes ever physically met.

Miranda and I bought a special picture frame for Lucinda's foster mother. On it is a "clothesline" with frilly dresses hanging on the line, and in the glass peers out my Lucinda, wearing her velvet dress and the lacy socks and Mary-

Janes in which her foster mother lovingly dressed our baby girl for a picture this past spring.

Even though I haven't yet met this woman, Lucy's foster mother, I know her heart. The pictures of Lucinda over the past thirteen months in her care speak volumes. It's one thing to be the birthmother and decide your child needs a loving home and family that you cannot provide, but it's another to be the "middle man," the person who cares for this baby, helpless and vulnerable, alone in the world, providing so much love and affection, attention and nurturing, knowing that one day this child will leave your loving arms and be whisked away by people living in another country that you don't know and haven't met.

It's a very difficult job, so selfless, so humane and loving. With this beautiful memento photograph of our Lucy, I also purchased for her with Miranda's help a bracelet of gold hearts. I hope when she wears it, she will know how much love we have for her, a woman we will always remember and thank God for bringing into our daughter's little life at the very beginning. After all, she is the person who gave Lucinda stability, care, and affection, the very first person who taught Lucinda to love and to laugh…

I can only imagine the sadness she feels this week, a flip-flop of the intense joy I feel as the minutes tick by, knowing the time is coming near when we will meet. She will lovingly present this beautiful baby to me, and I will gladly receive her. Our eyes will meet, mine promising her that the love and care that she began in Lucinda's heart I will continue to nurture for the rest of my life.

Lucinda has already had two mothers: the one who gave her life, and the one who cared for her in Guatemala, the only one she now knows. Soon she will be in the arms of the woman she will forever call "Mom," and that's me. I'm grateful for the first two. I have a swelling in my heart for these important ladies. They have given Lucy the chance to live a wonderful, happy, healthy, beautiful life. I will continue the love, attention, nurturing, and care that Lucy is accustomed to, this time forever.

Chapter 36:

We're Off To Guatemala!

Finally it was time to travel to bring home Lucinda! Dave and I packed our bags, said farewell to Miranda and my parents, and went forth on what we dubbed our "Operation Lucinda."

We flew in a windstorm from Newark to Atlanta and arrived in Guatemala City, Guatemala after dark on Saturday, November 30th. The next morning, Sunday, we were up at 6 a.m. for breakfast and then sat in our room waiting for the call from the lobby that Lucinda was downstairs!

By 8:30 a.m. we got a call from Maya, a representative from our adoption agency, saying the foster mother was planning to be in the Marriott Hotel's lobby at 10 a.m. It was finally going to happen! We were only hours away from meeting our daughter!

Dave and I tried to read or watch TV but that was impossible. Then the phone in our room rang around 9:30 a.m.; it was Maya, saying the foster mother had to change plans and would be in the lobby at 11 a.m. instead.

We were disappointed! We headed downstairs to the lobby to take a little walk and get out of our room for a short time.

After talking with the concierge outside the hotel, we headed back in at the very same time a Guatemalan couple with a baby was heading out the same doors we just entered. I noticed that the baby held in the woman's arms looked *exactly* like my Lucy!

So I said to the woman, "Crisna?" (That is Lucinda's Guatemalan name.)
And the woman said, "Crisna, si!" And she asked us, "You the parents?"
And we said, "Yes!"

Then everyone was smiling and hugging! To the nearest cluster of couches in the lobby we headed to talk.

I couldn't take my eyes off of Lucinda! She was just so beautiful! It was as if a picture just sprang to life!

Lucy's big dark eyes looked right into mine, and I talked softly to her, caressing her little hand. She was wearing a pretty flowered orange and white dress and a white cardigan sweater...and on her feet were the shiny Mary Janes that I admired from her previous photos.

I couldn't believe I was finally meeting my baby... She was just gorgeous and my heart was beating a mile a minute!

Somehow the agency got their signals crossed with the foster mother, so the adoption agency representative wasn't there to interpret. According to a Marriott employee acting as our interpreter, the foster parents were in the lobby waiting for us since 9 a.m.!

They were leaving when we, by some miracle, bumped into them. God's mysterious ways... We were in the right place at the right time!

The foster parents did an excellent job caring for Lucinda. It was apparent that she was greatly loved and cherished by them. I thanked Lucy's foster mother and father over and over for all of their kindness and love, and they simply nodded and smiled. There were tears running down Consuela's cheeks when she had to say goodbye to her little charge. When she handed me the baby, Lucy started to whimper, and I was just so sad witnessing this painful farewell. The foster father handed me their address and asked us to send them photos. We agreed, hugging them goodbye.

Lucy, now snug in my arms, just looked up at me and then at Dave. She wasn't crying. She was just staring at these two new people who suddenly took center stage in her little world. We three went upstairs to our room and quietly talked to Lucy, giving her a bottle prepared by her foster mother. Within minutes she was sound asleep in my arms.

It is scary having someone hand you a thirteen-month old child that you basically know nothing about! But Dave and I figured out what to feed her (trial and error in the restaurant), and we got the right milk for her bottles from the Pharmacia through the concierge at the hotel. Lucy gave us cues, and we followed them, and together we three became a team!

Even when she slept between us in the king size bed, we just couldn't take our eyes of off her. Finally, we had Lucy! Our Lucinda!

Monday our pink slip was in hand, and at 3:45 p.m. Maya came with her husband to the hotel to pick us up and bring us to the embassy doctor for Lucy's final medical check-up.

Lucy with her foster parents in the lobby of Guatemala City's Marriott Hotel, December 1ˢᵗ, 2003. Minutes later, tears streamed down Consuela's face as she said goodbye to the little girl she and her husband had cared for over a year.

Dave holds Lucy for the first time in the hotel. We are just so stunned. One moment we are childless in Guatemala, and now we have a toddler!

The very first photo taken of Lucy and me in our hotel room at the Marriott in Guatemala City just minutes after we said goodbye to the foster family. Lucy felt so light; now that I finally had her in my arms, I didn't want to ever let her go!

Having only been together for one day and one night, I knew the doctor's visit would be tough. No kid likes the doctor's office, especially one who is without a major support system—namely, one she calls Mom—to whom she can cling! My Lucy was with strangers going to the doctor. So I held her tight and we did our best together to get through the ordeal. There are no seat belt laws in Guatemala, so Lucy sat on my lap in the back seat of the car, and I held on to her for dear life.

First stop: a very seedy section of Guatemala City to get Lucy's photo taken. These little, tiny photos, required by the U.S. Embassy, are secured by the doctor onto the medical report. Photo taking is big business in Guatemala City, it seems, but there are not that many places to go to in the afternoon after the embassy's morning rush. This place seemed to be a twenty-four-hour joint, with shady figures hanging in and around the little dilapidated "shack".

A Doberman was on the balcony looking down at us, and while Lucy pointed her little finger at the dog, I held her tightly and stayed very close to Maya and Dave while we waited. The "photographer" pointed the camera at Lucy and the picture was done in seconds. It was fast and easy. After Maya paid the fee and received the tiny photos, we headed back into the car. I noticed Maya's husband locking and shutting each door fairly quickly. There were lots of men hanging around, looking at us. I was glad we weren't sticking around much longer.

Next stop: the doctor's office. We took the elevator and ended up in a very drafty clinic. We were ushered into a room where the nurse, who only spoke Spanish, told me in nonverbal ways to take off the baby's clothes. Lucy did NOT like that a bit. Then when she had to sit on the scale to be weighed, she howled! Dave and I had not heard her do a full-blown cry, so we were stunned at the powerful lungs this little one had!

The doctor came in shortly and told me to hold the baby in order to soothe her, and I really didn't think it would matter whether it was I or the nurse comforting her...to Lucy we were both virtual strangers.

But it DID matter.

When I held her, Lucy stopped crying! She clung to me and didn't want me to let her go. And in that very instant, my heart just melted. If one needed proof that bonding was going well, that was it for me! My baby needed me, and I was right there.

After some general questions, some medical observations (Can she see? Does she have a pulse? This medical exam was short and sweet and not very thorough...), we were free to dress Lucy and wait for the paperwork. While we waited, we got some prescribed cream for Lucy's cheeks. She developed impetigo (a minor skin infection) and needed a balm to stop the itching and heal the skin. In the waiting room Lucy walked, holding my hands. Dave and I discovered that that was her favorite activity: walking. Soon we had our paperwork and headed out the door and back to the Marriott.

Dinner was room service—cheeseburgers and fries for us and rolls and butter for Lucy—and the three of us sat in bed, eating, Lucy in the middle, nibbling at the French fries that she discovered she liked.

One more day and the adoption would be final...

At 6 a.m. the following morning, we were up and eating breakfast when we met Byron, our agency's facilitator, who was going to bring us to the U.S. Embassy. We reviewed together the mounds of paperwork, and Dave and I double-checked the money we needed to secure the final fees. We met Antonio, Byron's personal taxi driver, and we were back on the streets of Guatemala City.

At the U.S. Embassy, we had to empty almost everything from our bags. No bottled water... No cameras... No cell phones... No toys... No food... We were permitted one milk bottle for Lucy and not much else. We waited in the American citizens' line for about fifteen minutes, and then one by one North Americans were ushered inside. We were waved up and down by an electronic wand and then had to pass through a metal detector while our wallets and sweaters and even that one bottle were screened. Then an officer manually checked everything in our possession. The security was tight.

After clearing the security stop, we walked down a narrow aisle, through a metal turnstile, and then found ourselves outside again in front of the steps of the U.S. Embassy. There were armed guards with machine guns outside the gate that we previously passed to get to where we were. It was just one more reminder that we were out of the United States. The line of Guatemalan citizens waiting to enter the U.S. Embassy was long. Walking up the steps, we passed the American seal on the building and were greeted in the lobby by a big portrait of President George W. Bush.

Byron ushered us into a small room, capacity forty-nine. There was a line of people waiting. Many adults and children were sitting in chairs. Some were Guatemalan and some were U.S. citizens. Some were adopting, like us.

Strangely this place reminded me of both a bank and the Division of Motor Vehicles office back in New Jersey. The windows were numbered and there were glass partitions separating those behind the windows from those of us in the room.

After twenty minutes of waiting in the line, Byron went to a window and submitted our paperwork. Then we were called by name to another window where we presented our passports (two American ones and one Guatemalan one) and answered general questions. Then the woman asked us to raise our right hands and swear that what we presented to her was the truth. As we raised our hands and said the words, Lucy raised her little right hand, and the lady smiled!

She said, "Congratulations!" and that was it. After fifteen months of ups and downs, red tape and paperwork, delays and scares, pictures and deadlines, it was finally over. Lucinda Rubi Jean was officially our daughter, and she was now cleared by both Guatemala and the United States of America to leave her birth country and enter the United States to become an American citizen!

That night Dave and I packed our suitcases while Lucy peacefully slept, her last night in her homeland.

Early on Wednesday morning, after a quick breakfast, Lucy went with us in the Marriott hotel's shuttle bus to the airport. An incredibly long line awaited us, but after thirty minutes we were pulled out of line by a Guatemalan airport security officer who moved us to a special line where other families with babies were standing. That greatly cut down our waiting time. Lots and lots and LOTS of security clearances later, we found ourselves in a small waiting room with others heading to Atlanta, our port of entry into the United States.

The flight was on time, we boarded, and Lucy fell asleep in my arms. As we taxied to the runway, Dave and I looked out the plane window at the beautiful mountain ranges and distant volcanoes that we could see. Coming into the country, we were in the dark, but leaving, we could see the beauty of our baby's first home.

I felt sad, knowing that Lucy was too young to remember her year in Guatemala, that she was going to sleep through the momentous exit of her homeland, but at the same time, I felt warm knowing that our baby was coming home. She was one of the lucky ones. So many of Guatemala's poor never get a chance to live like she was going to live. I thanked Guatemala, Lucinda's birth mother, her foster parents, the U.S. government, and even my own mother who gave me life for allowing me to experience this incredible feeling that cannot be put into words.

And into the air we flew...

Lucy slept most of the way to Atlanta. She smiled and ate cookies through customs and immigration. Dave and I were running, running, running from place to place to place. We had to recheck our luggage, go through security again, and dash off to our connecting gate. And when we got there, the plane was already boarding. We were out of breath but so happy that we were on our last leg of the journey!

From Atlanta to Newark, Lucy ate the rest of her cookies and stubbornly stood in front of my seat in coach for which any frequent flyer knows is no easy feat!

As soon as we touched down, Dave took out our cell phone and called Miranda who was anxiously waiting with my parents for us at the airport. Before long we were heading down the aisle, and I saw Miranda and my parents with big smiles on their faces. Miranda was jumping up and down! She couldn't wait to glimpse her little sister in my arms. And with her big eyes, Lucy looked up into the faces of her big sister and grandparents. Waiting in baggage, Dave and my father collected the suitcases while my mother, Miranda, and I played with Lucy. Within minutes Miss Lucy was babbling, walking, and smiling!

We were home!

"Operation Lucinda" was a success!

Chapter 37:

Let Me Tell You About My Lucy…
December, 2003

Now that we're home from Guatemala and life is getting back to a new 'normal', let me tell you about my Lucy…

She has the biggest, most beautiful eyes, like a doe, as dark as black olives, with long lashes to frame them. Her cheeks are chubby and she lets me kiss them over and over and over again. On top of her round head are the most beautiful silky baby curls, black as night, wispy and adorable, curling just around her ears. And when Lucy smiles, she shows her four teeth, pearly white, and with those cheeks she looks like a happy chipmunk!

Lucy's skin is so soft, especially her round belly. She likes to inspect her toes when I change her diaper. Sometimes when she's in a playful mood she clicks her tongue and claps her hands and squeals loudly just to hear her voice! Her fingers are little, but they perfectly grasp little mini-marshmallows and cheddar cheese fish crackers.

When Lucy giggles, my heart dances! And when I put her to bed at night, rocking her in my arms, I can't help but think that life just doesn't get any better than this. God blessed me with a special gift, and I am cherishing her with all of my heart and soul.

For thirteen months Lucy was living in a foreign country with a foster family. Their customs and habits, language and foods were very different from ours here in the United States. So while most babies start to acclimate themselves to their families from the day of their birth, Lucinda had to do this twice in a lifetime.

She doesn't remember the first time when she was only two days old and went to live with the foster family in Guatemala. And she surely didn't know that December morning when she went with her foster parents to the Marriott Hotel in Guatemala City that she would forever be leaving them, the only parents she had ever known and loved.

Even though she didn't seem to react strongly to the loss of her foster mother whose tears streaked her cheeks when she had to say goodbye, Lucy has attached herself like glue to me. If I leave the room, Lucy whines. If Dave or Miranda holds her and I'm in the room, she puts her arms out and whimpers for me to take her in my arms. When she goes to sleep, it is safely snug in my arms while I rock her back and forth, singing softly in her ear. This is when she finds the comfort to let go and relax, sleep, and dream of more fun days to come.

She hasn't been home with us long, but I sense that she is afraid all of this will go away. She fights sleep as if she's afraid that if she closes her eyes, everything may be different when she opens them again. We may disappear just like the other family that disappeared. Everything that she knows may change. Her world could turn upside down again if she doesn't keep a close eye on things.

Am I exaggerating? Projecting? Imagining? I don't know. But I do know that the experts in the adoption field say there is a traumatic loss that adopted children feel at different stages of their lives. There will always be a before and an after for Lucy.

All I want for her right now is to feel tremendous love, safety, comfort, and a sense of belonging. I want her to be happy. So does Dave. When Lucy wakes up at 2 a.m. in her crib, crying with her eyes closed, still asleep as if dreaming a bad dream from which she cannot awaken, I immediately scoop her up in my arms and bring her back to our bed where she sleeps in between us until morning. Dave moves way over to his side, and I move way over to my side, and in between us sandwiched between pillows is Miss Lucy, sound asleep. Dave and I look at each other in the morning and smile as we gaze at the snoring little nugget of love that is lodged between us. She's been through enough, and so have we.

And then there's the sisterly bond that is forming between our girls. Miranda adores her little sister, and Lucy adores her big sister. At dinnertime, the two like to laugh at each other. Lucy will throw something on the floor and laugh, and Miranda breaks out in giggles at the sight of this little munchkin laughing at her own mess. This causes Lucy to giggle, too, and that causes Dave and me to laugh.

Lucy likes to taste everyone's food. She sits in her high chair at the end of the table, directly across from Dave, and acts like a queen. When she puts out her little pudgy hand for a taste, you better give her a pinch of what you're eating! And if she likes it, you better be ready for seconds and thirds. In a show of generosity, Lucy, too, likes to share her food with everyone, and it doesn't matter to her if her daddy has to get up from his chair to walk over to hers in order to taste the mashed up mess that is gripped in her extended hand just for him. Her eyes dance when you like what she has to offer. Her smile is our dessert.

Miranda asks what we're having for dinner in the mornings so she can look forward to what she can offer her little sister from her plate. And that's usually when she's giving Lucinda the marshmallows from her Lucky Charms cereal during breakfast. Miranda is smitten.

Toys have completely taken over our family room. Everything that can be put up high is jammed on a shelf. There are fingerprints on the coffee table and mouth prints on the glass door, but we've never been happier. Lucy is just another word for love. And we four keep smiling, feeling like the luckiest people in the world to have each other.

Lucy—just one week after leaving Guatemala
and entering the United States.

Chapter 38:

A Baby Eating Pizza?!

Lucy only has four teeth, but it feels as if her gums are lined with steel. I know this because I foolishly put my finger in Lucy's mouth when we were playing, and when her jaws clamped shut around the tip of my finger, my eyes started to water; I pulled with all my might to get my finger free from harm's way. Luckily the tip of my finger is still attached to my body! This explains why, at only fourteen months of age, Miss Lucy can eat almost anything!

When Miranda was that age, I followed "the rules." I introduced all the baby foods that Gerber and Beechnut made, spacing each meat, vegetable, and fruit accordingly to know if she had any allergic reactions to any of the foods she ate. Whatever the pediatrician said, I did. Sometimes I followed my mother's and grandmother's advice, but most of the time, I went by "the book."

With Lucy, all that has changed. I knew we were going to be swimming upstream when we were in Guatemala during our first meeting with our daughter, and I asked her foster mother what Lucy ate; she responded, "Everything."

Dave and I looked at each other. We wondered if that meant she likes all the various kinds of jar baby food, that she wasn't a picky eater, or that we could just buy whatever we desired for her and she would eat whatever we gave her. "What an incredibly easy baby Lucy was going to be," I thought! It's a good thing I brought with me a box Gerber rice cereal! Now Dave and I would have to find the nearest pharmacia (supermarket) to buy jars of baby food during our stay in Guatemala...

Well, that's not exactly what "everything" meant.

When we gave Lucinda her first bowl of rice cereal, she spit out the first spoonful and refused another bite. When we gave Lucy some Gerber pear food from the jar, she spit that out, too, making a sour face. Ditto with the rest of the jar food we bought. So here we were in a foreign country, living temporarily at the Marriott Hotel with a child we just met who, at age 13 months, needed to eat, and we were clueless what to feed her besides the Gerber Arrowroot Cookies that I brought for snacking!

With great trepidation we headed to the Marriott's buffet table, ready to experiment with "real" food for breakfast. Since I never started Miranda on table food until she was much older, I was really out of my league here, so I was ready for anything. I truly hoped that the waiters and waitresses knew baby CPR…just in case.

Dave and I quickly discovered what 'everything' meant:

Croissants

Cheese

Bananas

Potatoes

Scrambled Eggs

Pancakes

Watermelon

It was fun experimenting with foods. Little Lucy sat in her high chair and casually took in her little hand whatever bits of food we gave her, tasting them and, when she discovered she liked them, she opened her mouth wide and extended her hand for more. At one point she got exasperated with our speed and technique, grabbing a chunk of banana from the table, and Dave and I smiled when we saw her eat it almost as if she was eating corn on the cob! She was so little and the food was "real," not the mashed up version of food that we were accustomed to feeding babies.

When I looked around at the other adopting families with babies at their tables, I was happy to see that all of them were eating from their parents' plates, too. We weren't "bad" parents after all! Even though we were breaking the traditional rules that we learned in North America, we were learning that in Central America there were different rules to follow.

And this became a theme for us: be flexible and open-minded. Experiment and try new things. Adapt what you know and what she is accustomed to. Don't be afraid to be different. When one adopts an international child, he or she has to be open to all of these things. Rigid parents are big on control; those of us who adopt children from foreign countries have to give up that control early on.

After all, for months and months my baby girl was being raised by people I didn't know and I wasn't privy to their ways and means of child rearing. All I knew was that there were people out there taking care of Lucinda, and I hoped for the best. I was praying that Lucy was living in sanitary conditions, was drinking formula, was being bathed and diaper-changed regularly, saw the doctor for routine visits and immunizations, and was receiving lots of love and attention. Not knowing wasn't easy, but I had to put Lucinda in God's hands.

So the germ-a-phobe who eleven years ago sterilized every single nipple and pacifier, who promptly discarded bottles of formula not consumed within thirty minutes, who bought fancy bath tub devices for head and back support and safety, who only bought brand names of baby products because surely they were the best (no generic for my baby), who wrote down precisely when, what, and how much Miranda ate and drank at each meal—that person is now in 2004 introducing foods like pizza, macaroni and cheese, mini-marshmallows, cheddar cheese goldfish, Spaghettio's with franks, chicken lo mein, and sliced turkey to her baby who loves every bite!

My how things change if we let them…

Lucinda is as happy as a clam. She loves to eat. And she is thriving. At our first doctor's appointment, when I mentioned to the pediatrician what Lucinda was consuming at meals, I thought I would get a stern lecture. I winced, telling her what I had been feeding my precious cherub, but instead of consternation, I got reassurance. The doctor said that internationally adopted children are raised differently than those in the United States, and these anomalies are to be expected. She said not to change anything—that Lucinda had been through enough change—and to continue doing what I was doing, that Lucy was healthy and adjusting well to life in North America.

I left the doctor's office with Lucy in my arms, smiling, thankful for the big and small things I continue to discover in this wonderful world of adoption that I've entered. It's been one month since Lucy has been home, and my heart is filled with joy. First I fell in love with Lucy in pictures, and now, after getting to know her personality, mannerisms, and appetites, I adore her even more. It just keeps getting better and better…

Lucy feeds her big sister a mini-marshmallow.

Chapter 39:

She's Healthy!

During the waiting phase of the adoption, I kept imagining Lucinda in my mind. She was always healthy and smiling. When it was time to go to Guatemala and bring her home, my heart skipped a beat when Miranda's pediatrician told me about all the possible diseases she could have contracted, living in Central America.

Yellow Fever...Hepatitis...Parasites...Bacterial Diseases...

He told us to be careful when we were in her country, and I cringed a bit, thinking more about my baby being there for over a year than what I could pick up during my few days in Guatemala.

I reviewed Lucinda's photos when I got home, and she certainly appeared healthy and clean. The medical updates didn't reveal any illnesses, but then again, when you're adopting internationally, there are so many unknowns. Soon I'd find out.

At the Marriott in Guatemala City the first night of our union, I inspected Lucy from head to toe in the bathtub. Lucy seemed apprehensive about getting into the water, as if she had never had a bath in a tub before. Perhaps she hadn't. But once she realized she could splash the water with her hands and that the water felt really good after a long day stuck in diapers and clothes, she enjoyed herself.

Lucy appeared clean and healthy.

The immunization book that her foster mother gave me showed that she had all of her immunizations on time. Other than some dry skin patches, my baby appeared the picture of health. But we all know appearances can be deceiving.

At the doctor's appointment in Guatemala, a mandatory procedure at the end of the adoption journey before the child enters the United States, the doctor was concerned about some of the skin "lesions" that Lucy had. We showed him the antibiotic cream that the foster mother gave us, and he inspected it. Then another doctor came in and examined Lucy. We were concerned, of course, but then the doctor handed us another prescription for antibiotic cream, saying Lucinda must have contracted an infection and a rash developed that spread by her scratching. He told us to keep her very clean and to trim her nails short to prevent more spreading, and, like the gospel, we did just that.

When we arrived home in New Jersey, it was a Wednesday. On Thursday, Lucy, Miranda, and I headed to the pediatrician's office for Lucinda's first visit. Some adopting parents go to adoption specialists, but I felt comfortable going to our pediatrician's office where the doctors were well versed in international adoption and adopted children's medical issues. After an initial check-up from head to toe, the doctor made us an appointment with a dermatologist to look at that rash. She also wanted us to get a sample of Lucy's blood drawn, a urinalysis done, and have stool tested.

I was glad that the pediatrician was being cautious and conservative. Sometimes adopted children from impoverished countries aren't thoroughly tested because in the doctor's office they appear clean in their middle class clothing with their middle class families. However, it's imperative to have all the testing done to know exactly how healthy your child is and what needs to be done to ensure continued good health.

Lucinda's first day in America was an odyssey. At 1:00 p.m. we saw the pediatrician, and at 3:00 p.m. we saw the dermatologist. He looked at the skin spots (with Lucy fast asleep on his examination table) and concluded that she had impetigo, a contagious skin infection. He prescribed another antibiotic cream, and off we went to Quest Diagnostics to have the blood work and urinalysis done.

At 4:00 p.m., Lucinda was in my arms, now groggy but awake, and into her little arm went a needle to draw two vials of blood. I cannot tell you how excruciating that was for ME let alone Lucy. I had to hold her still, and into my eyes she looked, crying and miserable. I kept reminding myself that this was for her own good, but my heart still hurt for my innocent babe.

In the waiting room sat Dave and Miranda. After hearing her baby sister crying, Miranda started to cry, too, and soon I was comforting both girls after the whole ordeal concluded.

The pediatrician's urine bag was detached and the urine specimen was collected, and we were given a stool "kit" to complete at home over the next four days. As the scientist of the family, Dave, a chemical engineer by trade, took charge of the collection of stool. I saw him reading directions and adding and shaking things in test tubes. It was a yucky job, and, despite the "doody" jokes from Miranda and me, he did well.

Within days the results were in.

The pediatrician's office called, and when I saw their number and name on our caller ID, I was nervous. The lab tested for HIV, syphilis, Hepatitis B and C, Ova and parasites, Giardia Antigen, and bacteria infections. What if something was found? What if Lucy was sick, really sick, and I was about to be told? What if my bubble of happiness was about to burst? What if, after traveling all this way to start her new life, Lucy was in for a battery of medical testing? I braced myself and answered the phone.

The nurse said Lucinda's test results were good; only slight anemia was detected, and that was most likely from her diet in Guatemala. I was instructed to buy baby vitamins with iron and mix a dropper-full into her milk bottle in the morning. That was it! My baby was healthy! I can't tell you how relieved I was.

One month later, Lucy and I headed back to the pediatrician's office. It was tuberculosis-testing time, and two additional vaccinations were scheduled. Many international children receive what is called a BCG vaccine for tuberculosis, and in the United States, this tends to cause a positive test result. If that happens, a chest x-ray is recommended, and if that comes back negative, then an anti-tuberculosis antibiotic medication is prescribed for the next nine months. Oh, boy, I thought. Please let my baby be spared.

A needle prick in the left arm and one shot in both legs later, Lucy and I headed home. That was a Friday. On Monday we had to return to have the TB test "read" by the doctor. All weekend long, I kept looking at Lucy's left arm, feeling it with my fingertip to see if there was any reaction to the test. A "pimple" would appear if she tested positive for TB exposure. To my heart's delight, there was nothing.

On Monday the doctor looked at Lucy's smooth arm and declared a negative TB reading. Yeah!!! That meant Lucy had no exposure to tuberculosis and would not need any further testing done.

After calling the Center for Disease Control and finding out that Guatemala's immunizations were reliable, the pediatrician said the magical words, "Come back in three months. Lucy is now on a 'normal' schedule, just as if she was born right here in the United States." Music to this mother's ears…

*December 4th, 2003—this is the first picture taken of
our family of four!*

Chapter 40:

Welcome To A New Year!

It seemed like an eternity, but finally my family is complete.

Right now, all snug in her pink blanket sleeper in her crib sleeps Lucinda, finally home after thirteen months in Guatemala. Miranda is in the basement playing Play Station 2 with her dad, both of them absorbed in the drama and the fun, and I am in front of the computer, quietly contemplating how lucky I am to have it "all."

I have a great husband, two wonderful, loving daughters, parents, grandparents, and other close relatives who cherish me, friends who make me smile, and a God who watches over me. I am healthy and happy going into a new year.

My resolutions for 2004...

I resolve:

To never take for granted my two beautiful daughters and my kind, caring husband.

To update the photo albums often in order to capture the special moments of our family.

To try to remember how it feels to be eleven, so I can give Miranda every ounce of my compassion, love, and understanding! I adore her!

To shower love and affection on my baby girl Lucinda Rubi so she thrives in the years to come. She truly is my miracle!

To stop grinding my teeth. The adoption is over.

To share my love of reading with my girls.

To give the cats a treat now and then. They deserve something special, especially during their patience as Lucy learned to pet the cats "nicely."

To call and write to my friends both near and far. They mean so much to me.

To not be afraid to try new things, to experiment, to see life in new and different ways.

To enjoy the little moments and remember that that is really what life is all about.

To enjoy an hour with Dr. Phil or Oprah and not feel guilty!

To be true to myself.

With Lucy now home, I feel a peace in my heart and in my soul. I can finally sleep again, the insomnia gone, the fears and 'what ifs' no longer occupying my mind. Dave, Miranda, Lucy, and I are a family, finally united, and it feels as if we've been together forever, even though it has been less than a month. It seems as if we can't stop smiling, laughing, and giggling at the funny things we do and say to each other. I think all four of us in our own unique ways learned in 2003 what is really important in life. Thanks to so many, we have so much.

2004, welcome!

Chapter 41:

The Squiggly, Wiggly Girl In The Middle

It's been six weeks since Miss Lucy has come home. She has adjusted well to the change from Guatemala life to life in the United States, so well, in fact, that she doesn't want to take breaks to "recharge her batteries." Sleep? It takes too much time, I think she thinks.

When we were in Guatemala City at the Marriott, Lucy fell asleep within thirty minutes of meeting us. I gave her a warm bottle to drink, and right there in my arms, she fell fast asleep. I gently put her on the bed, and there she napped, angelic, and my heart swelled with love. That evening, after giving her a bath, Dave and I were amazed at how quickly she fell asleep. And she slept through the night right between us! It didn't matter, after all, that the Marriott ran out of cribs; Lucinda was a good sleeper! This pattern continued the few days we were hotel-bound and getting acquainted.

Then we came home. Need I say more?

In New Jersey Lucy didn't seem to mind the cold, winter air, the purple princess blanket sleeper that she now wore at night, or the new noises and faces and things she was first encountering. She smiled that first night, happy to be surrounded by so much love and attention, and she didn't want it to end.

Yep, she did NOT sleep much that night. I figured it was just because of all the change, so Dave and I shared our bed with her. All night I just kept looking at her anyway, amazed that finally my baby girl was home!

The next day, she was raring to go. Nap? Nope. She didn't want to slow down. A few zzzz's in the car seat going to and from the doctor's office would suffice. At night, she fell asleep in my arms when I gave her a bottle, and I gently put her into her crib. She snored loudly, and I couldn't help thinking she resembled a drunken sailor, blissfully happy and content.

But sometime around midnight, she was up! Standing in her crib, holding the bars, she was whimpering, and it grew louder as I waited to see what she would do. How could I let my Lucinda cry? I waited a whole year to finally be with her! Within minutes I was right there, picking up my baby and holding her soothingly in my arms. She put her head on my shoulder and fell fast asleep, that is, until I tried to put her back in the crib. As soon as her curly locks touched the mattress, she was wide-awake, holding up her arms for me to pick her up once more. This happened about three times before I finally decided that I needed to get some sleep. So I brought her back to bed with me, and as soon as her head touched my pillow, she was out like a light.

This pattern continued. I discovered that she would take a nap during the day if I would lay down on my bed with her. So I did, and we both caught some shut-eye. Of course, that meant that NOTHING was getting done around the house, because I was right by Lucy's side all day and all night…

Despite the house being in disarray and the laundry piling up, we were doing well, bonding and delighted to be together. But soon Dave was complaining. How often could he sleep just a few hours and still be awake during business meetings? Little legs were hitting him in the stomach at all hours as Lucy twisted and turned in her sleep. At first it was delightfully cute, but now….

Off to the store I went. I bought pillows—three of them—one rolled pillow for the top of her crib by her head and two soft chenille pillows for the sides of her crib. This was in addition to the crib's bumper. Why all the padding? I thought in her sleep Lucy would think she was sleeping between us. She liked pillows—she was hogging ours—so "operation pillows" began. And just to appease the little one, I also bought a pacifier. Perhaps that would "pacify" her in the middle of the night.

So with pillows and pacifier, Lucy went to sleep in the crib and slept until 4 a.m. that first night! Dave and I were so excited! It worked! Of course, I was up at 1 a.m., startled that I didn't hear Lucy whimpering; I went into her room to make sure she was ok. Her arm across one of the pillows with the pacifier in her mouth, Lucy was sleeping! Success!

Now I won't lie to you and say that this works every night. Some nights I can't seem to get Lucy into the crib at all. I discussed this, of course, with the pediatrician. I was expecting to hear her tell me that I needed to let Lucy cry it out, but instead, the doctor's words were very wise and thoughtful. She said, "Since we don't know what her life was really like in Guatemala on a day to day basis, and we don't know where or with whom she slept her first thirteen months of life, perhaps it isn't a problem that she wants reassurance and comfort in the middle of the night. After all, it isn't a problem unless you say it's a problem, right?"

I thought about that. As long as she is sleeping and we are sleeping, there really is no problem. I let myself off the hook. So Lucy wasn't sleeping all night in a crib. So what?

For now, the pacifier and pillows in the crib continue. That and coming to Lucy's rescue in the middle of the night, reassuring her that we're still here and love her. There's nothing more special than seeing those big eyes of hers flutter open in the morning and a smile appear on her face, happy to see me and her dad, happy to start a brand new day. As for Dave and me, we're adjusting well to the new sleeping pattern in our lives. We don't get uninterrupted sleep anymore, but we've gotten used to the squiggly, wiggly girl in the middle.

Chapter 42:

Hands Off My Mom!

It's interesting having two children who are ten years apart. Just the other day Miranda wanted a makeup lesson because *everyone* at school, she said, was now wearing makeup. So while I gave her a crash course in Eye Shadow and Blush Application 101, my fifteen-month old Lucy was trying to take off her blanket sleeper. She had it completely unzipped, and exposed was her flowered undershirt that she wrestled with. No luck freeing herself from the confines of clothing. So at 8:00 a.m. that morning, my half-undressed little one and I waved bye-bye to my sixth-grader who proudly showed off to the neighborhood girls her sparkling eyelids. What a dichotomy!

In some ways my girls are very similar. They are both affectionate and love to hug their mom. But this can bring controversy. We discovered this over the weekend when Miranda and I sat down together on the couch and held hands while we talked. Lucy toddled over and started to stare at us…then she started to yell…then she tried to push our hands apart. "Hands off *my* mom!" she seemed to be saying in baby speak.

Miranda was shocked! She couldn't believe it! "She's *my* mom, too!" my eldest said to her little sister, laughing at the burst of emotion this affection was causing. Miranda again held my hand, and again Lucy forcibly pushed our hands apart. Then Miranda hugged me, and that made Lucy really mad! All nineteen pounds of her tried to push our bodies apart, yelling the whole time until Miranda and I were untangled. In an attempt to appease both girls, I lifted Lucy onto my lap and we did a "group girl hug;" Lucy tolerated this for a moment, and then, again, she pushed Miranda away. "Hands off *my* mom!" was the message she was trying to convey.

When I looked into Lucy's stern face as she was defending her claim on me, I couldn't help but feel proud and happy that my little one's bond with her mother was so strong. After thirteen months in Guatemala with her foster mother, she had to start all over again with a new female caregiver, and she seemed to instinctively know that this one was for keeps. Or maybe she thought the first one was gone, so she better fight harder and stronger to keep this new one. Whatever the case, I reassured both of my girls that I loved them both, kissing both of their soft cheeks, and holding both of their hands in mine.

It's amazing the amount of love that we feel for our children and that our children feel for us. In a topsy-turvy world where so much changes so fast, it's wonderful to know that some things never change. It's important for Miranda to know that despite adopting a daughter, I still adore, cherish, and fiercely love her with all of my heart. I told her how proud I am of her to share her parents.

After ten years as an only child, it took a great deal of guts on her part to open her heart and willingly let someone else love the mom and dad she loves who love her. Sure, biological siblings do this all the time, but they don't have a choice. In our case, Miranda had her eyes wide open. For her it was a conscious choice. We discussed as a family our desire to adopt a child, and at age ten, Miranda was very much in the driver's seat with us when it came to making decisions.

I remember feeling an incredible rush of love for her when her eyes softened as she thought about how special it would be to have a little sister (because a brother for her was out of the question), how wonderful it would be for a little person without parents to have parents and opportunities like she had. My Miranda is a very generous, caring girl, and she felt secure enough in her world to give us the o.k. to move forward and open our hearts to another daughter. That is very special indeed.

When Miranda comes home from school, she kisses her little sister; Lucy smiles at "Da" (her name right now for big sis), and her face lights up! It's playtime, she thinks, immediately running to the nearest wall so they can play hide-and-seek. When Miranda is practicing piano, Lucy listens, thrilled when her big sister finally lets her sit on her lap and they play the keys together. And mealtime is fun for both girls because they share food and laughter.

There is a mischievous, loving glint in their eyes when they look at each other—true sisters despite the age gap! Their love for each other grows daily. It's heartwarming to watch.

So until Lucy gets old enough to realize that her mom is also Miranda's mom, Miranda will giggle when Lucy tries to pry us apart, and Miranda will say "Not fair!" when Lucy is exclusively in my arms. It's great to have the love of two very different daughters, one in sparkling eye shadow and one in disposable diapers. They will both realize in time that there is enough love in my heart to cherish them both forever.

March, 2004—the sisters in matching shirts!

Chapter 43:

Adoption Is An Option

Several months ago, I was horrified to hear the news that a young boy was found dead in a storage bin in a Newark, New Jersey basement. He and his two brothers were living with a woman and her teenage son, caretakers designated by the boys' mother who was in jail. The woman caretaker and her son were arrested and charged with the child's death; the two other boys were removed from the home and placed in foster care.

How could this happen? In this day and age, how could a boy just disappear and no one notice for several months? How could a grown woman, a mother herself, hide a dead boy's body and hope no one would ever find him?

Of course, there was a lot of public outcry about this tragedy, and the Governor of New Jersey immediately asked for an investigation. Did the Division of Youth and Family Services (DYFS) know about these boys and their living situation? What would become of the brothers? Families from all over the tri-state area called DYFS and volunteered to adopt the two surviving siblings.

Before this sad case could fade from memory, another hit me between the eyes. An older couple with grown children, pillars in their church, who legally adopted boys whom they previously fostered, who received state money to subsidize the boys' living situation, was accused of starving the adopted foster children in their care. Late one night their nineteen year-old was rummaging in the neighbor's trash cans for discarded food; someone called DYFS. This young man looked more like a nine year-old boy. He was emaciated and small.

All of the boys were taken out of the home and hospitalized, the couple were arrested and charged with a variety of crimes, and the case was put on the docket for trial.

A few days ago I awoke to a morning radio newscaster saying there were more children under the care of DYFS now than ever before, and it's not a secret that there aren't enough workers to adequately supervise the placements of all these children. In a related story, the Governor's wife is going to be part of an advertising campaign to promote the Safe Haven Law that legally protects mothers who, anonymously, drop off their unwanted infants at police stations or hospitals. This comes after the deaths of fourteen infants: some by strangulation, some by drowning in toilet bowls, some by hypothermia…

There are permits and classes and tests in order to drive in each state, but there are no permits, classes, or tests to pass in order to become a parent. It's the most important job anyone can do—without a doubt, the most demanding and trying job any of us may ever tackle. So why are parents-to-be so inadequately prepared?

As an adoptive parent as well as a biological one, my heart bleeds for the children who fall through the cracks, the forgotten ones, and the "unlucky" ones who don't stand a chance to live a good life. They by no fault of their own find themselves without parents who can care for them the way they deserve to be cared for. As time goes on in our civilized, highly sophisticated society, the numbers of parents who cannot care for their own children should be waning, not increasing.

Drug addicted mothers often abandon at birth their drug addicted infants. Teenage girls in denial of their pregnancies give birth, sometimes in the suburbs where we ourselves live, and discard their babies in trashcans or toilets. Remember several years ago that teenager in New Jersey who gave birth to a baby in the bathroom at her prom, literally threw away her newborn, and then went back to her date and danced the night away?

So many times abusive and/or alcoholic parents who were most likely victims of their own parents' abuse or illnesses take out all of their hurt and frustrations on their very own innocent children. Shaking a baby to "shut up" and stop crying is a permanent, lethal mistake for some who find themselves caretakers of babies out of necessity versus want.

The poor just seem to get poorer and become homeless, unable to feed, clothe, or shelter themselves properly. And with crime in society so rampant, many convicted offenders leave children behind when they go behind bars to do time. That's how the state gains custody of so many children.

There are thousands of children in the foster care system throughout the nation in need of family life, love, and guidance. Sometime in the span of these children's young lives, they lived in horrendous conditions and/or experienced trauma from which they may be scarred for life. Maybe their mothers got pregnant and gave birth to these children for whom they could not adequately care, love, and/or protect. or these women found themselves in precarious situations or unfortunate circumstances that caused them to let go of their children's hands way too soon.

And where are the children's fathers?

As a society, we need to fix the family. We need to instill into our children, especially teenagers, the old fashioned ideals of our parents and grandparents who taught us to care for each other, to take responsibility, to work hard, and to always protect the family.

Life is precious. It's a gift. And we are all responsible to not let each other down. For those not fortunate to have parents or grandparents with high values and ideals, it's time society taught them how to heal, grow, and be responsible in order to break the cycle of abuse and neglect.

Pro-life? Pro-choice? It doesn't matter, because once a child is born, he or she needs care. Once a child is born, either the child is raised by his or her biological parent(s) or someone who can provide stability, love, and care adopts him or her. Whichever the case, the child's needs *must* be met. It is not acceptable to fail children, damage them, kill them, or send the survivors of such abuse and neglect into the world defenseless and helpless after years of being stuck in a bureaucratic, overwhelmed system.

When I look into Lucy's eyes, I think about the woman and the man in Guatemala who gave her life. They were not married or together, even, by the time Lucy was born, and they were both extremely poor. Lucy's birthmother made a decision in her baby's best interest. After carrying in her womb this baby girl, she decided that this child of hers needed loving parents and all the opportunities in life that she deserved. Unselfishly she gave her baby the gift of a life not just by carrying her to term but also by consciously deciding that she was an unfit parent. She took responsibility, even if that decision caused her heartache. And Lucy is a happy little girl, "lucky," some people tell me, to be loved and wanted so much. But I say there was no luck involved, just responsible people acting responsibly and compassionately in the best interest of a child.

All children need a chance to be loved and cared for, to grow and learn, to smile and laugh, and to dream of a better world to which they can contribute and make a difference. The ones that we don't read about in the newspapers shouldn't be considered lucky for having what all children should have every day: stability, care, love, happiness, safety, clothing, shelter, education, and opportunity.

Society needs to digest this and open its eyes before we fail more children by not doing anything to protect them. Adding more DYFS workers isn't the long-term solution—but fixing the family is. Perhaps it needs to be shouted more loudly and clearly that, faced with an unwanted pregnancy or dire circumstances that prevent a mother and/or father from caring adequately for their child, ADOPTION IS AN OPTION. Outside the United States this seems to be heard loud and clear—why not in America?

Chapter 44:

Elmo To The Rescue

As a former college English major and high school teacher, I have a passion for books and the written word. I am the type of person who walks through the library and sees old friends on every shelf. At the bookstore I take the time to touch the spines of the books that took me along for incredible rides and taught me lifelong lessons. By my bed there is always a book I'm in the middle of reading and one waiting in the wings for my attention. A book 'wish list' that I compile is next to the computer. Enough said.

Before Miranda could even sit up by herself, I would put her on my lap in the rocking chair and I would read to her. Dr. Seuss was definitely one of our favorite authors. In Miranda's room were shelves of books, some just waiting for her to become developmentally ready to tackle them. When she was Lucinda's age, Miranda patiently sat on my lap and let me read to her. When she got older, she finished the sentences Dave and I would read on the pages of her books. She was born loving books.

Eleven years later, Miranda still loves to read, although she does have to be prodded into a book every now and then. There's no better gift one can give a child than the love of reading. It lasts a lifetime.

During the long adoption wait, I so looked forward to bringing home Lucy and exploring the world of books together. Would she need bilingual books? I was prepared to buy Spanish Dr. Seuss if need be... *Goodnight Moon, Guess How Much I Love You, The Giving Tree*... So many 'friends' were back in the baby room, waiting, like us, for Lucy.

When Lucy arrived, I soon discovered that this little one didn't have the patience to sit and let me read to her! She was active, energetic, and so ready to explore and inspect every little inch of her new dwelling. Every time a book was introduced, Lucy would glance at it, then get up and go for another exploration of the kitchen cabinets.

Next she discovered that it's fun to rip paper, so up high went Miranda's beloved Dr. Seuss books for when Lucy was older and could appreciate the written word; down low went the toddler board books that could take a beating and still retain their story. But, alas, Lucy just wasn't that interested in books.

Not one to give up, I detoured in a different direction. *Sesame Street*, I thought, would pave the way for Lucy's love of learning. So every morning at 7:00 a.m. we welcomed PBS into our family room while Lucy drank her first bottle of milk. But, well, you guessed it—even *Sesame Street* couldn't keep Lucy still. I let her play but kept the show on in the background. Then, when I realized that *Sesame Street* was only on TV once a day, I decided to purchase some VCR tapes to play in the afternoons.

With repetition, the *Sesame Street* theme caught Lucy's attention. Whatever she was doing, she stopped and looked at the screen when she heard "Sunny day sweeping the clouds away…" crooning from the electric box. Sometimes I would sit her on my lap and we would watch some *Sesame Street* together, enjoying Big Bird and Elmo. In this way she was exposed to letters and numbers and concepts vital to her development and intellect. I am not promoting children watch countless hours of TV, nor am I promoting TV over books, but when it comes to *Sesame Street*, I think it's an educational oasis that allows children to think and enjoy learning new things. Yes, it's rare today to have such a show, but let us count our blessings that *Sesame Street* is still going strong since its 1969 debut.

A few weeks after her homecoming, Lucy and I journeyed to the public library. She was interested in running up and down the aisles and taking books off the shelves more than she was interested in sitting on my lap and letting me read anything cover to cover. But it was a start.

A few weeks after that, the whole family ventured out on a snowy day to the local bookstore, one of our favorite places. It was Lucy's first visit, so we were excited to show her the big, colorful, child-friendly children's section, thinking maybe, MAYBE she'd be interested in letting one of us read to her. She immediately discovered the platform where many story time readings are held, and she played with her big sister on the stage. I zipped over to the toddler board book area, determined to find something that would just knock Lucy's socks off and get her curious about the written word. Every now and then I'd bring one over and try to entice her into a story, but she was more interested in that stage.

When we were ready to leave, Miranda came over to me with a little board book and said, "I think Lucy would like this one." I looked at it, and on the cover was *Sesame Street*'s Elmo. *Elmo Loves You* was the title, and there was the furry, red, loveable monster bursting out of a heart. I glanced over at the table where she found it and saw several Valentine's Day themed books for children. After reading the story I decided it just might be the book we've been looking for, the one that would introduce Lucy to the wonderful world of reading. Excited, Miranda and I purchased it without doing a 'test read' on our 'guinea pig'.

At home, Lucy's eyes sparkled when she saw her friend Elmo on the cover of the book. "Do you know who this is?" I asked her, smiling. She came forward and took the book in her hands, then sat down and opened it! I sat next to her and read as fast as I could (because Lucy doesn't turn pages slowly), and we actually got to the end of the book, her very first book! I was so excited! And what came next was astonishing. She picked up the book and brought it to me to read to her again! So we read that book over and over and over again.

The next morning, amid all the board books on her shelf, Lucy picked up *Elmo Loves You* and brought it into the kitchen while I was getting breakfast ready. Looking down and seeing her holding the book up, I stopped everything and sat right down on the linoleum floor and read to her. I read that book four times in a row! And every time we got to the end, where Elmo asks for a kiss, Lucy leaned forward and gently kissed Elmo. Not only was she enjoying the rhythm of the words in the book, but also she was comprehending the story!

Now, two weeks later, I notice that Lucy is opening more and more of her books, looking through the pages, sometimes babbling to herself as if she's reading. She still won't sit through the reading of other books, but she will for Elmo. She gets excited and giggles when she hands me the Elmo book, knowing the wonderful story that awaits her. The repetition, the rhyme, and the familiar *Sesame Street* characters entice her, and she can't wait for the kiss.

Elmo Loves You gives me hope that one day Lucy will blossom into a reader, one who will enjoy adventures with friends she will meet in print. It only takes one book to open up that world! Thanks to *Sesame Street*, Lucy is learning and adapting to the English language.

*Lucy is awestruck when she meets her idol, Elmo, at Sesame Place in
Pennsylvania. Normally very independent, Lucy clung to me without
taking her eyes off of "Melmo!"*

Chapter 45:

The Dark Circles Said It All

Just when I think I have studied Lucy backwards and forwards, something happens that makes me remember that we've only been together for less than three months. It is the most frustrating situation, trying to understand what a toddler is trying to express without the benefit of words. Last night was one of those difficult times for both of us.

Typically Lucy and I go upstairs to her room around 7:30 at night to rock in the rocking chair. I give Lucy her bottle of milk and we cuddle. Within twenty minutes Miss Lucy is snoring, the bottle almost empty. I quietly pick her up, give her a kiss, and gently lay her in her crib. That's her sleep routine...usually.

Last night, I gave Lucy the bottle and rocked her in the rocking chair, but Lucy seemed unusually wide-awake. A few times she seemed as if she was slowing down and possibly closing her eyes, but I was fooled. When she started squealing and babbling twenty minutes into the nightly ritual, I knew this was not going to be an ordinary night. Of course, babies are human beings, not robots. I remind Dave and Miranda of that when they look shocked and alarmed that Lucy isn't asleep by 8 p.m. Normally Lucy is very true to her schedule, but not tonight.

Instead, I took Lucy into my bedroom where it was quiet and dark, and I lay down with her, hoping she'd fall asleep. Instead, she rolled one way, then the next, straining upward when she came close to my face to give me kisses on my cheek. Who could resist that? I had to reciprocate, and the two of us were giggling and kissing in the dark.

9 p.m. and Lucy was still awake...

By 10 p.m. Lucy was grouchy...and so was everyone else in the house.

Miranda wanted to go to sleep; Dave wanted to watch some TV and relax. But Lucy was noisy and cranky. Despite rubbing her eyes, a definite sign of tiredness, she kept trying to get something—lint or a piece of hair? —out of her mouth. I tried to help her, but I wasn't successful either. Even drinking water and sucking the pacifier didn't help. I was running out of ideas to calm her down.

I rocked her in my arms. I held her in my arms and walked around the house. I sang to her. At times she calmed down, and sometimes she even put her head on my shoulder, but the fussiness continued. Then the crying started. What was the problem?

Dave and I tried to understand what she was trying to tell us. A light bulb went off in both of our heads at the same time—a tummy ache! Maybe her stomach was bothering her and she needed a dose of gas medicine to ease her pain. It was worth a shot. So we ventured downstairs, hurrying to the diaper bag to find the medicine. Within seconds, one squirt with the dropper was dispensed into Lucy's mouth, and within minutes she was quiet again, weary but seemingly relieved and not in pain.

She went right to sleep. Before we got to the top of the stairs and into the bedroom, she was snoring. Exhausted, she slept right between Dave and me. I was awake for the next hour, the adrenaline still pumping. It seemed as if every hour on the hour throughout the night I was checking Lucy to make sure she was ok, breathing, warm…all those "mom" things.

Around 4:30 a.m. she was softly whimpering, something she sometimes does in her sleep that may be attributed to the adoption and all the changes she's been through in such a short amount of time. I rubbed Lucy's back and whispered in her ear, "I'm here, Lucy; you're ok." Normally this worked, but this morning her crying escalated. Into my arms I tucked Lucy. Downstairs we went for more tummy medicine. In minutes, she was smiling, and the two of us quietly, in the dark, watched Lucy's favorite *Sesame Street* CD on the couch. With Lucy on my lap, I lay back on the couch and closed my eyes. It's physically draining, at times, caring for little ones when they don't feel well.

Within a couple of hours Dave went to work, and then Miranda ventured to the school bus. Both cats went to their designated bedrooms of choice to snooze. To start our day, Lucy and I ventured back upstairs and climbed under the covers. We didn't need common language to discuss that. The dark circles under both of our eyes said it all.

Chapter 46:

Milestones

A call from a social worker came last week. "Please make a list of your daughter's milestones since she's been with you," the woman said, and we agreed to meet in a couple of weeks for her court-appointed visit to our home.

In the state of New Jersey, one has to "readopt" a child to legally change her name and obtain a United States birth certificate. What does this mean? Lots of paperwork, of course! An adoption report, copies of all of the adoption documents, a copy of Lucy's Guatemalan passport and alien registration card, and a list of Lucy's milestones, medical appointments, and immunization record since she's been home with us in addition to a visit to our home by a licensed social worker are all required.

A few weeks after returning from Guatemala with Lucy, Dave and I obtained the legal paperwork and filed in court our readoption petition; a judge then granted us a court date for April 1st. He appointed a social worker to come to our home and meet with us in March, see Lucy, and observe our interactions and living conditions. The social worker then writes a report, and if the judge is satisfied that everything is legal and proper, Lucy becomes "official" at our April court appearance. That's a major milestone, indeed, because it marks the "end" of the adoption process that we began two years ago.

So it's time for me to list the milestones and accomplishments of my baby girl.

Like any proud mama, I can rattle them off at the tip of my tongue:

Lucy began walking one week after coming home to live with us.

Three more teeth have joined her other four pearly whites.

Lucy recognizes her name and points to herself in a family portrait.

In less than three months, Lucy grew one size larger in clothes and in shoes.

Lucy now drinks from a sippy cup; she can also drink from a straw.

When she eats breakfast in the morning, Lucy feeds herself yogurt with a spoon.

Lucy has had three immunization shots and two wellness visits to the doctor since coming into the United States.

Lucy says "Da" for Miranda. She waves her hand hello and goodbye.

Every Saturday morning Lucy socializes with other toddlers at a children's gymnastics class.

It's amazing to read this list and realize all of this happened in just two months!

And then there are the tender family milestones that help forge the person Lucy is becoming. For example, I will never forget the day I asked Lucy to throw a napkin away in the trashcan, an object of her fascination, and she did it! She looked at my face, listened to what I was saying, then turned around, toddled to the trashcan, lifted the top, and threw in the crumpled napkin. Then she turned around to look at me with the biggest, proudest grin on her face. I clapped and said, "Yeah!!!!" and she clapped too, smiling at her own achievement.

That night I asked Lucy to throw another napkin away, and she was delighted to do so, amazing Miranda and Dave who, wide eyed, also clapped. Sure, it's like a puppy trick, but to a little girl who was immersed in the Spanish language and Guatemalan culture for over a year, it's a significant milestone in language and understanding. After her trashcan milestone she added the following:

When I say, "Let's go change your diaper, Lucy," she runs over to the baby gate at the bottom of the stairs that leads to her room and patiently waits for me.

"Here comes Daddy and Miranda!" gets Lucy to drop whatever she's doing and run to the front door where she greets her father and big sister with hugs around their big legs.

"Are you hungry?" I ask Lucy, and if she is, she goes right over to the refrigerator and waits for me to open it. She tells me she's done eating when she holds the high chair tray in both hands and yells. (We're working on that one…)

"Can you give me a kiss?" Lucy is not that generous when it comes to kisses, but she will sometimes give a sweet, tender kiss on the cheek to her mom, dad, and sister when asked. And she always has kisses to give her stuffed animals (on their noses) and our two cats (who tolerate it to the best of their feline abilities).

"I'm going to get youuuuuuuuuuuuuuuu!!!!" makes Lucy giggle and run around the house, her arms, legs, and body facing forward, her cherub face smiling, looking back.

Lucy loves to point to a framed family portrait we have on the shelf. It was taken the day we became a family of four; there we sit, on the couch, all smiling and happy. Lucy loves to point her little finger on the glass at each face, and I say who they are. When she points to herself, she smiles. Now when I say each person, she points to that particular face. I am always touched when she does that, because it means that she knows her family. And when she looks at that picture, she knows that that's *her* family.

And then there's the bathtub. When I first met Lucy at the Marriott Hotel and gave her a bath that first night, she cried, afraid of the water. The second and third night she learned how to splash, and then she loved taking a bath! When we came home to New Jersey, Miranda and I added bubbles to her warm water oasis, but to our dismay, Lucy was afraid. When we moved the bubbles to show her that indeed her feet were still attached to her body, she laughed. Then she touched the bubbles herself and a bubble bath queen was born! She learned trust in the bathtub, and I was touched by her sweet innocence and wide-eyed wonder at the new world she was encountering. The bathtub was a big milestone in our development as a two-some.

Meeting her four grandparents was a big moment, too. That first night she stepped foot on American soil in Newark's Liberty Airport, she met her grandmother and grandfather. Then a big snowstorm threatened to blanket the state, and my parents flew back to their home in Florida the very next day. Still, she met my parents and they had the opportunity to see her come home. Likewise, she met Dave's parents a few weeks later at their home in New Hampshire, Lucy's first road trip. There she discovered that there are lots of buttons to push on the electrical gadgets at Nana Jean's house. But she also enjoyed all the new toys wrapped just for her.

Next stop was Massachusetts where Lucy met my grandparents. Her great-grandmother was in the hospital, recovering from a fall, but the big smile on her face when she finally saw Lucy in person, holding a Get Well balloon in her little hands, made the moment special, one I will always remember. Lucy was nervous; the lady who was grinning at her was in a bed hooked up to wires… As long as I held her in my arms, Lucy was content.

After the hospital visit, we went to the nursing home where my grandfather lives, and he was delighted to meet his newest great granddaughter. He rummaged through his bedside drawer to find the secret stash of cookies he hides from the nurses. He presented Lucy with a cookie, and as she looked into his warm eyes, he smiled, broad and wide; he was very happy. He kissed her little cheeks, and Lucy was amazingly patient and calm despite never having met him before.

Sometimes life's connections make us aware that we are in the presence of special, kind people, and I think Lucy sensed that when she met her grandparents and great grandparents. There are more relatives to meet, specifically baby cousins who are only a few months younger than she, whom she will meet in a few weeks. She is discovering that there is a family outside her base family who love her, too. And that feeling of connection is indeed an important milestone.

So many new experiences, new words, new foods, new faces… Lucy has had a full sixteen months of life. But I think her greatest milestone to date is feeling safe and warm in the arms of her mommy, the lady who looked right into her eyes on that December day in Guatemala, a woman she had never seen before, who spoke the international language of love that Lucy recognized right away. There was something special about this person, Lucy sensed. And when their eyes met, they instantly fell in love with each other. And that love is in full bloom. Apart for so many months through so many adoption obstacles, they are now together, forever, and they both realize that. And for them both, that is the greatest milestone of all.

Dave's parents Larry and Alice Jean with the girls.

With my parents, Deeny and Howard Shore.

Chapter 47:

Ah, Spring!

OK. So it's not *officially* spring yet. Someone has to tell that to Mother Nature, who today, the first day of March, sent the birds flying high into the pale blue New Jersey sky. The sun is shining, warming the brown, matted grass, nudging it to wake up and grow green again. And that air—ahhhhhhhh! There's nothing better than inhaling clean, fresh outdoor air after being cooped up indoors all winter! I don't care what the calendar says... I am welcoming spring!

And so is Lucy. This morning, at 8:30, we put on our coats and headed outdoors to celebrate the nice weather! I unfolded the "Cadillac" stroller, the padded, shock-absorbent model that Dave and I bought many months ago, and seat-belted a wide-eyed little girl who couldn't understand why we weren't getting into the car. This was to be a brand new experience for her.

Comfortably situated in the carriage, Lucy sat back and enjoyed this new way to ride. It was more relaxing, not as fast, and peacefully quiet. There was no music except for the chirping of the birds. Lucy's black hair looked shiny in the sun's rays; strands of her baby-fine hair were gently blowing in the wind. It wasn't warm, but it was nice not having heat blowing from a vent into our faces. We liked the cool air on our cheeks, the warmth of the sun naturally heating us.

Ah, spring!

No longer was Lucy stuck in the middle of the back seat, strapped into the cumbersome car seat. Now she was sitting in the front seat, enjoying the view. When she looked up, she saw the never-ending sky and wisps of cottony-white clouds. She had to squint her eyes to see the sun. When she looked down, she saw pebbles on the sidewalk. I stopped the stroller so we could closely examine the pointy pine needles on the pine trees. The other trees, merely naked sticks, have buds on their branches. Lucy looked at the different houses, the pretty welcome signs, the occasional dog on a leash, a patch of snow melting… There were so many new things to think about and discover on this nice morning walk.

And then we stopped at the park. In a small clearing sat the swings, neglected for several months, gently swaying, inviting us to reintroduce them to the world of fun. Lucy thought it strange that we were stopping and getting out; she could tell this wasn't home!

In the baby swing, Lucy looked around, not knowing what this strange contraption she was sitting in was, not sure she liked it. Then I gently pushed her and she swung back and forth, her little hands gripping the swing handles, her eyes wide with wonder and delight. Her curls glistening in the light of the day, and Lucy smiled, happy to experience a swing at the park for the very first time.

So there we were, swinging and strolling in the New Jersey warmth of the first day of unofficial spring, enjoying the solitude, the beauty, and the feeling that life outdoors is about to burst at its seams. I remember those sad days in autumn when I walked these same streets, thinking how beautiful the colorful leaves looked, longing to share the walk with my Guatemalan baby. Lucy's adoption may have been longer-than-average, but she's experiencing all that I dreamed for her right here, right now… and my heart is as full as Mother Nature's.

Ah, spring!

Chapter 48:

Looking At Life Through Baby Eyes

It's disheartening to pick up the newspaper these days and read about suicide bombers in Baghdad, rock-throwing Palestinian boys, angry Haitian rebels, insider trading scandals, terror cells …the list goes on and on. It's amazing to watch war on CNN and then switch the channel to see Ernie and Bert singing on PBS' *Sesame Street*. Such dichotomy… Then I try to imagine what life must look like through the eyes of sixteen-month-old Lucy, an internationally traveled toddler who has been a U.S. citizen since December. It makes me smile to think of what she would say:

"Why do the big people love it when I push the buttons on the toy phone, but when I try to push the buttons on the *real* phone, they take it away and put it up so high that I can't reach it anymore?"

"It's fun to play at the kitchen table with a spoon and fork, but it's easier to eat food with my fingers. I don't know why the big people don't try it."

"What's the point of wearing clothes? Naked feels so much better!"

"If I were a big person who could control the knobs of the bathtub, I would take a bubble bath all day long — not just for thirty minutes at night."

"The big people like it when I nod yes and no to their questions, but they get upset and agitated when I point at things and yell at them for not getting me what I want when I want them. They should really try to understand my language like I'm trying to understand theirs."

"Why does Dad get annoyed on Saturdays and Sundays when Mom puts on my *Sesame Street* DVD? There aren't any catchy songs on his sports shows anyway…"

"Miranda's school backpack and purse have zippers and snaps and buttons, but when I try to open them, she shrieks and yanks them away! Geez… I share *my* toys with *her*."

"Those cats like it when the big people pet their soft, silky fur, but when they see me coming, their eyes get big and they jump over the baby gates so I can't touch them. Isn't that discrimination?"

"Why does it take those big people so long to change my diaper? I have blocks to build, toy buttons to press, stuffed animals to hug… I wish they would hurry up!"

"I hate seat belts! Why do I need to be restrained in the car, in the highchair, and in the stroller? The United States is all about freedom, right?"

"Beds are soft and bouncy. Why doesn't anyone else jump on the bed with me? Why do they always want to close their eyes in the dark?"

"That flusher on the toilet is sooooooo cool! I wish I could flush over and over and over again, but Mom says once is enough."

"I would love it if Big Bird and Elmo could jump out of that box plugged into the wall and play with me! Dad gets nervous when I try to bang on the glass 'window' to get their attention."

"My mom likes to type on the computer, but when I try to type, too, she hits a button real fast and the screen goes blank. Why does she shut it off just when I am ready to help her with her writing?"

"What's the deal with all this kissing? Don't the big people know that we small people don't want their lips all over our chubby cheeks all day and all night? I'm not safe even when I'm sleeping. Sigh…"

Once upon a time we were all innocent, inexperienced, and ignorant to the ways of the world. Perhaps if we all turned on PBS to watch *Sesame Street* each morning, took a two-hour nap after lunch, and frolicked with bubbles in the tub at night, we, too, would see that the world is big, filled with limitless possibilities, and all people, no matter skin color or age, religion or nationality are uniquely beautiful.

If Lucy were old enough to understand the sound bites and stories broadcast daily on CNN, she would most likely ask me, "What happened to make the big people so mean to each other?" Whenever I see and hear about all the disrespect, dishonor, and destruction going on in the world, I often want to ask that question, too.

Jim Henson, Fred Rogers, Shari Lewis, Captain Kangaroo, you are all sorely, sorely missed…

Chapter 49:

A Weekend At The Castle

We went to Massachusetts for the weekend to visit with relatives. As long as there were plenty of cookies, toys, and a pacifier handy, Lucy was happy on the four-hour car ride. She scared off her big sister Miranda who begged to sit in the front in case Lucy had a tantrum, so I was delegated to the back seat. Lucy and I held hands and napped on and off. It wasn't bad at all. Miranda and Dave listened to a book on tape for entertainment, but *Sesame Street* songs interrupted the story every now and then in order to appease the little girl in the backseat—she ruled the car with an iron fist!

We checked into the hotel, a Sheraton in the shape of a castle. When I was a little girl living in Massachusetts, I always thought this hotel was magical. Miranda instantly fell in love with it. "We're here!" she said, excited to be on "vacation" even if it was just for three days and two nights. The best part for her was that there was an indoor pool, and we promised Miranda that we'd go swimming, but not right away…and that didn't go over so well.

Once in our room on the fourth floor, Lucy instantly found the remote control to the television set. So the TV went on and off, channels changing erratically, as we opened our suitcases and hung up our clothes. Then we took a quick drive to my grandmother's new apartment. After more than sixty years in her house, Nana sold it and moved into a senior citizens' housing complex. Having recently recovered from pneumonia induced by a back injury that kept her laid up in the hospital, she was happy to be healthy and back home again. She was even happier to see family. My parents were visiting from Florida, so all of us hugged and kissed hello, happy to be together again.

Lucy looked at all of these people skeptically. After all, she met her grandparents and great grandmother only once before. Miranda thought it

193

was funny to see Lucy so quiet and cautious, but within thirty minutes she was back to her old self, running around and pushing buttons on the TV. She found the candy jar filled with chocolates, a staple at my grandmother's house, and that put a smile on Miss Lucy's face.

That night, Miranda wanted to go swimming, but after the long car ride and all the visiting, we decided we were too tired. Tomorrow, we told her. Miranda clung to that promise.

The next day after picking up my grandmother we headed to the nursing home to visit with my grandfather. His memory comes and goes, and, sadly, this was the first time he kissed me hello and asked me my name. That was a jolt, though I knew it would eventually happen. My grandfather is 89 and frail, a shadow of the robust man he once was. But he is still my Zadie, and I was happy to see him. Miranda entertained us with a concerto on the grand piano in the parlor where we were sitting, while Lucy enjoyed opening and shutting the big parlor doors.

There in that room sat four generations: my grandmother and my grandfather, my father (their second born son) and my mother, Dave and me (my father's oldest and only daughter), and my two girls. It was one of those times when everyone was smiling and talking and laughing—I just wanted to freeze the moment and stop time in its tracks.

But, alas, I was unable to do such a thing, so I cherished the moment, conscious of making it a lasting memory to share with my daughters many, many years from now when we reminisce.

After lunch we headed back to the castle. Was it finally time to swim? Grandpa and Miranda went in search of the indoor pool. Miranda was full of energy and excitement, but she returned deflated and disappointed. "It's crowded," she said, flopping herself onto the bed. There's no room at all to swim.

Grandma tried to infuse some enthusiasm into the situation, and within an hour Miranda was agreeing to go swimming. Grandmothers sure have a way with words. So on went the bathing suits. Lucy didn't like the feeling of her light blue mermaid bathing suit—it felt tight around her chubby legs and arms—but she looked adorable!

To the pool we went.

By the time we got there, the water had cleared, making Miranda grin from ear to ear. She loves to swim, loves to swim with Grandpa, and the highlight of her trip was to swim with her little sister for the very first time!

Lucy looked at the pool stoically, not registering fear or excitement on her little face. Miranda tried to coax her into the warm water right away, but Lucy was content just looking. When she was ready, I held her in my arms and we went into the shallow end together. It was funny, because she really didn't react at all to being in the pool. She felt safe in my arms.

After watching her big sister swim under the water like a fish, Lucy was tired, so she put her head on my shoulder. Soon we went to dry off and talk with Grandma; Lucy was happy sitting on my lap all bundled up in a thick, warm towel. She watched her sister and grandfather swim.

Then Miranda enticed little Lucy back into the water, and the craziest thing happened—Lucy fell asleep on Miranda's shoulder! Miranda walked laps in the pool, thrilled to have her little sister snuggled into her neck in the water, Miranda's favorite place to be.

By the end of the weekend, we spent some time with my two brothers and their wives who officially welcomed Lucy into the family. They thought she was so beautiful and small...a real princess! And of course Miranda, long-legged, blue eyed, and sweet as sugar captured everyone's heart as she always does. Lucy met her cousin Matthew who just turned one. Face to face, the toddlers stared at each other. Then Matthew touched Lucy's hair and smiled; they became fast friends. Miranda laughed at their antics.

We departed the castle the next morning and headed back to New Jersey full of magical memories of a weekend well spent.

Chapter 50:

Loving Another's Child

I stole away from the house early on Saturday morning to get my haircut. My mother asked how long it had been since I had it cut, and honestly I couldn't say. Life with a little one is just all-consuming! But the mirror told me that my hair was out of control, and a cut was in order.

I went to the same salon but had a new beautician cut my hair and wax my brows. She was a very friendly lady, in her early fifties, who definitely knew what she was doing. I was in good hands.

As we made chit-chat, I mentioned that I have two daughters, and one my husband and I recently adopted from Guatemala. She wanted to hear all about the process, what made us decide to adopt, how difficult the waiting was… She was hungry for information.

As I was lying back in the chair, having my eyebrows plucked and waxed (what a luxury!), the beautician said something interesting. She told me that she had trouble with her own pregnancies when she was younger. She had several miscarriages and a stillbirth. I didn't know what to say. It's always so sad to hear about other people's heartbreak, and I hear about it often when adoption is the topic.

She confided that she and her ex-husband thought about adoption, but she nixed the idea. "I didn't want to raise another woman's child," she said. I was tongue-tied hearing that! And the tears welling up in my eyes were appropriate from the plucking experience, but I think there was more to it…

Honestly, I never, ever think of Lucy as someone else's child. She's mine. From the moment she was a thought, I loved her. When I downloaded her first picture and gazed at my Guatemalan beauty, I melted. She was definitely mine, and I never, ever questioned that.

So to hear someone utter those words "someone else's child" made me really think. I imagine there are those who feel that way, that adoption isn't an option because the child isn't "theirs," but that makes me question what makes a child your own.

Miranda came from my body. She lived in my womb for nine months and I carried her everywhere we went. We were one until she finally made her way into the world. I remember looking at this little pink infant and thinking, "So that's who you are." You're the one I prayed for when I wanted to have a baby, the one who was kicking me many nights when I was trying to sleep, the one who hiccupped over and over again in the second trimester, my first born. That was my Miranda. Before her birth day I hadn't seen her, but I felt her, and I surely loved her.

That is the same way I fell in love with Lucy. From the moment I thought about my second baby, I loved her. No, she didn't physically grow in my womb, but she lived in my heart. And for thirteen months I waited to touch her, to hold her, to sing to her, to love her with all of my being. I didn't feel her kick or hiccup, but I imagined it. The first time I saw Lucinda smile, I was elated. And when little teeth appeared in the monthly photo updates, I beamed. There was never, ever a question of whether or not Lucy was mine. Of course she was mine.

I like to say that God wanted to challenge Dave and me. He delivered Miranda to us the "easy and direct" way, but Lucy somehow ended up in Guatemala, and God led us to her. Instead of a c-section, we had fingerprinting and mounds of legal paperwork to complete. Truly, it was just as painful. And the first time I held Lucy in my arms I felt the same indescribable rush of love that I felt when I first held Miranda. Really.

The beautician did a wonderful job. Before I left, she said, "You know, I really wish I was as mature as you are at your age; now I wish I had a child."

The more people hear about adoption and see first hand that it works, the more "sold" on the idea they become. And if more and more people adopt, especially the international babies who are truly desperate, what a wonderful world it would be.

Chapter 51:

Her Time To Shine

Throughout the adoption, from beginning to end, Miranda has been very patient. An only child for many years, Miranda suddenly was sharing the spotlight with a sibling. Once Lucy came home, everyone in the family faced a big transition, but no one faced a bigger challenge than Miranda.

A sixth grade student in the last year of elementary school, Miranda is going through changes. During the preteen years, girls go through a transformation, and Miranda and her friends are no exceptions to the rule. With those hormonal changes come mood swings, insecurity, and occasional defiance. One minute Miranda is happy, loving, and sweet and the next she is moody, argumentative, and angry. On top of that there is the pressure of school: projects, tests, and homework. Lastly, there is social peer pressure from which no girl escapes. Where you shop and what you wear and even the size of your house all matter all of a sudden. Her friends' opinions really count. My Miranda is growing up.

And with all this new turmoil and angst in her life comes a toddler from Guatemala who wants attention, love, and affection. Whatever Miranda does, Lucy wants to do; whatever Miranda has, Lucy wants to hold. If Miranda laughs, Lucy giggles. If Miranda cries, Lucy whimpers. When Mom and Miranda "have words," Lucy mimics the tone, yelling baby talk to get her voice heard. Suddenly Miranda's world has turned upside down! Her parents, her house, her pets—they are no longer solely hers. And she is suddenly learning that babies aren't all fun and games; sometimes they can be bothersome and annoying!

So I wasn't surprised when Miranda asked me not to bring her baby sister to the talent show. "She will make noise and embarrass me, Mom!" pleaded my oldest. I knew how "big" this event was to her.

Typically shy and quiet, Miranda surprised everyone when she decided to try out for the school talent show. She rehearsed her piano piece for weeks and was very nervous the day of try-outs. But she and her duet partner were successful.

Miranda was so excited when she discovered that she and Susan secured a spot in the show that she called me late in the morning on the school payphone to tell me her name was on the list. "I'm in the show, Mom!" she proudly stated, hungry for mother-praise. And I lavished it on my girl. I was so happy that finally, after a very long time, it was Miranda's turn to shine in the spotlight all by herself. For several months she patiently weathered all the attention lavished on Lucy by family and friends. It was finally her turn to shine!

And she didn't want Lucy to steal the spotlight.

I didn't blame her. But at the same time, how could I not bring Lucy? She is part of the family. And she is little, not used to being with a babysitter, not accustomed to being away from her parents or sister. And, yes, I admit, her mother is not ready to take that big separation step yet.

I promised Miranda that I would be vigilant with Lucy, that I would make sure that she didn't make a peep, that she would not embarrass her on her big night. Reluctantly Miranda agreed, focusing her attention instead on what she would wear.

For several weeks, every Tuesday and Thursday after school Miranda and Susan practiced on the piano, rehearsed with the other student acts, and prepared for the show. Every time I picked her up from rehearsal, Miranda glowed with pride. This was a really big step for Miranda. Coming out from the shadows, she was ready to be noticed.

The night of the talent show we arrived at school at 6:30 p.m. Dressed in a long black skirt and white shirt, wearing nylons and new "cool" shoes bought just for the occasion, Miranda was ready. Nervous, too. As soon as she saw Susan, she was off, handing me her jacket as she ran down the hallway to the music room.

We three settled into our seats—second row near the piano. Lucy, in her blanket sleeper, enjoyed the pre-show fun. She banged on the metal chairs and smiled at the ladies admiring her in the next row. When she spied the piano, she made a quick dash over to the keys, tapping a few as she stood on tiptoe, mischievously smiling at Dave. Her dad laughed. Lucy sure was a character. Even the principal came over to introduce herself to Miss Lucy. Soon the lights blinked and it was time for the show to begin. Miranda was in the second act, so we had an hour before we would see her on stage.

To my surprise, Lucy stayed awake throughout the entire first act. She drank some milk from her bottle, ate some crackers, and even enjoyed chomping on her pacifier, a real treat since that only comes out when it's time for her to go to sleep. Clutching her stuffed cat, Lucy sat on my lap and enjoyed the dancers and singers. When the pianists performed, Lucy was a bit antsy; we assumed that was because she was immune to piano playing after hearing Miranda play every day and every night. But Lucy still wasn't making any sounds, and that was good.

At intermission the crowd dispersed into all different directions. Mothers were talking to impatient children who were eager to talk to their school friends, little kids were running in and out of the auditorium, fathers were fiddling with camcorders and cell phones. It was pandemonium as the first act ended and the second act set up.

But in all that hustle and bustle, Lucy saw Miranda. By the door Miranda was standing, a big smile on her face, talking animatedly with a group of her friends who came to see the show. Lucy made a mad dash to her sister, scrambling to position right in front of her and instantaneously raising her arms to be held. Miranda bent down and picked her up, holding her in loving arms. Miranda's friends were so envious! They asked to hold her, but Lucy would not let go of her big sister, and that made Miranda beam with pride! Dave and I watched our girls, smiling from afar.

When the lights flickered, signaling everyone to get back into their seats, Miranda scrambled over to me and handed me her sister. "Mom, please don't let her make any noise!" she pleaded once more, looking worried that Lucy seemed unusually awake at this late time of night.

"Don't worry!" I told her, giving her a kiss on the head. "She'll be fine. Good luck, kiddo!" I whispered, watching my eldest run toward the stage.

Two more acts, some dancing and singing, and then it was time for Miranda to perform. Dave jockeyed for position with the camcorder, and I held Lucy even tighter in my arms. She had her pacifier firmly implanted in her mouth. The audience clapped when Miranda and Susan came from backstage and took their places on the piano bench. Then the melodious sounds of *"Beauty and the Beast"* filled the auditorium, and I watched Miranda in all of her glory gracefully play the piano.

I had a huge smile on my face. "That's my girl!" I thought, so proud. My heart was overflowing with love!

That's when a high-pitched squeal came from the little girl I was holding.

"It's Miranda!" is what Lucy wanted to say, impatiently trying to get my attention as she wildly pointed toward the piano. Despite the dim lights and the row of people in front of us, Lucy recognized her sister and the song.

Lucy was so excited! I immediately clamped my hand over her mouth, whispering to Lucy that, yes, that was Miranda, and we had to be very quiet while we listened to her play the piano. Lucy was wide-eyed and smiling!

Despite intense concentration and jittery nerves, Miranda heard the squeal. I worriedly looked at her face, praying that Lucy didn't alter Miranda's performance. Instead, Miranda smiled, acknowledging the noise, and continued to play. She knew that it was her sister's way of saying, "I love you, Miranda!"

In all of her innocence, Lucy was showing everyone how proud she was of her sister. And despite her preteen moodiness and unpredictability, Miranda was mature enough to know and accept that about her sister. Was I proud of her!

After the song ended, the audience cheered. Looking up and taking a bow, Miranda was grinning ear to ear. I know that image will stay in my memory forever: in center stage looking beautiful, more grown up than I had ever seen her, Miranda was confident and happy. And at the same time, her parents and baby sister were deliriously proud as we clapped for her wonderful performance. It was Miranda's time to shine. Out from the shadows, my girl was in the spotlight!

Chapter 52:

Readoption Day

On December 1st, 2003, we physically met Lucy in the lobby of the Guatemala City Marriott and held her in our arms for the very first time; on April 1st, 2004, just four months later, we held Lucy in our arms as we entered the Monmouth County Courthouse in Freehold, New Jersey, to meet with the judge in his courtroom and formally readopt our baby girl from Guatemala.

Readoption varies from state to state. In New Jersey, a child may be granted a name change and receive a state birth certificate if the adoptive parents fill out the necessary paperwork (there is *always* a mound of paperwork!), pay court fees, consent to a home visit from a court-appointed social worker, and appear in court. Even though one can use an attorney, Dave and I chose to save some money in the costly adoption process and fill out the readoption paperwork ourselves. We filed them in February.

The social worker came to visit us on a Monday morning in March. Dave stayed home from work just for the occasion; the social worker wanted to see the parents interacting with the child in order for her to write her report.

Lucy was as sweet and as active as ever, and I was glad she didn't stick her hand into the social worker's purse that was placed on the floor near the couch during the interview. We answered lots and lots of questions. What are Lucy's sleeping patterns? How is she adjusting to home life? What developmental milestones has she hit? What type of personality traits does she exhibit? What was the trip to Guatemala like? How is the bonding between Lucy and her sister?

The social worker was pleased that Lucy "kept her distance" and viewed her as a stranger of whom to be wary. I never thought about it until that moment, but a child who is adopted at the age of thirteen months goes from the only family she has ever known to virtual strangers. Old enough to form relationships and bonds, the child is traumatized, so it's important for the child to bond with the adoptive family. She needs to know that she is loved and cared for by these people. If this doesn't happen, then the child will go to anyone; she will never be wary of strangers.

Obviously it is imperative to the child's safety and emotional development that bonding happens, and in our case, it obviously had. Lucy was very curious about the lady sitting on the couch that didn't belong to the house, and she really wanted to see what was inside that purse, especially the cell phone that was sticking out, but she resisted the temptation. Ah, our girl was healthy and right on track!

We had to pay three hundred dollars to the social worker's agency after the visit and wait three weeks for the social worker's written report (a copy sent to the judge) deeming us a good placement for Lucy. It just makes you realize that adoption is not freely accessible to anyone who wants to love a child in need of a home and family; one has to be able to afford to adopt privately. Volumes can be written about the cost of adoption…

The big day in April finally arrived. We picked up Miranda from school at 2:00 p.m. and headed to the courthouse. Lucy was in a new dress, pretty polka dotted tights, and pink shoes just for the special occasion. True to form, there was no bow or barrette in her curly black hair. Lucy likes to be *au naturel*, and there was no fooling around with her hair on April Fool's Day, Readoption Day, or whatever this day was called here in the United States. In the car she clutched her favorite stuffed kitty as she sat in her car seat and listened to the songs of *Sesame Street* playing on the car's CD player. And on to the courthouse we drove.

After passing through the metal detector, we headed to the judge's courtroom and waited outside for our names to be called. Other families were smartly dressed, waiting their turns for readoption. A family coming out of the courtroom caught my eye. The mother was holding the hands of her Korean-born sons, one six and one twelve months old. They were dressed identically in khaki pants and green sweaters; penny loafers covered their feet. The father was walking hand-in-hand with their daughter, a girl who appeared to be about nine years old, wearing two pigtails in her hair, a dress, and dress-up shoes. She was dark-complected, perhaps from Haiti or Africa. We spoke briefly before they exited and we entered the courtroom. The woman asked about our experience with Guatemala, because she and her husband are looking into an adoption from that country next. What a beautiful family they had, all possible through various forms of adoption. I bet they will be back to readopt another child next spring…

In the courtroom, we four were asked to sit at the table opposite the judge. Two assistants and a security officer sat on opposite ends of the judge's large, wooden, raised desk, placing the judge higher than the rest of us in the courtroom. He wore a black robe and spoke into the microphone "for the record."

Miranda's eyes widened at the formality of the moment. I think she thought she might be arrested if she did anything unacceptable! Lucy sat quietly on her big sister's lap. No more babbling came out of her mouth when she looked up at the judge. It reminded me of the *Wizard Of Oz*—the awe-inspiring wizard today was the judge who was to grant us our wish—to be a family.

Dave and I stood, placed our hands on the Bible, and promised to tell the truth, the whole truth, and nothing but the truth.

The judge asked me questions:

What was your relationship to the child before the adoption?
"I did not know her," I answered.
Did the child have any material possessions?
"No. She came with nothing."
How did the child come to the United States?
"My husband and I traveled to Guatemala City to bring her back with us."
What is the name that you wish to call this child from this point forward?
"Lucinda Rubi Jean."

He explained to us that once the adoption was finalized, Lucy would have the same rights as Miranda, our biological child. And with that, after a few more questions, a review of the social worker's report, and a question to Dave, the judge declared our family a "proper placement for the child," and granted the adoption. He congratulated us on becoming a family.

I smiled a big smile. Of course, for the last four months we have been living as a family, so this wasn't anything new, but it was finally formalized, cemented in "the record" of the court in the United States of America. NO ONE could sever our ties now. And that just felt so, so good. After the roller coaster we'd been on, it felt nice to step off.

I kissed the top of Lucy's head and smiled at Miranda. Dave and I let out a sigh of relief. Later we agreed that it felt like the time we were pronounced husband and wife. Symbolically, we were united as a family.

The judge's assistant asked us if we'd like to have photos taken with the judge. We said yes, handing her our camera as we climbed the stairs to be on the judge's platform behind the big, imposing desk. The judge shook our hands and congratulated us again, smiling at each one of us. We posed and smiled and said goodbye. As a reward for good behavior, the judge's assistant offered Lucy and Miranda lollipops. Lucy's eyes danced as she selected one from the hundreds in the canister.

And off we went, down the hallway of the courthouse, toward the parking lot, to drive home and live happily ever after.

April 1ˢᵗ, 2004—Lucinda's readoption in Freehold, New Jersey. Our family poses with the judge who moments earlier congratulated us on becoming a family.

Epilogue

Finally "Home"
May, 2004

Saturday morning I awoke to the sounds of the instrumental version of "Rock-a-bye Baby." This morning I awoke to singing. No, I wasn't dreaming, but it did denote a dream come true!

Let me explain…

Most parents take it for granted that in the mornings their toddlers will wake up in their cribs and play. Eleven years ago, Dave and I were no different. By the time Miranda was one and a half she would sleep through the night, and we used to love listening to her babble, sing, and play with the toys in her crib when she woke up in the morning. We assumed that would happen with Lucy, too, when we daydreamed about her coming home, but that's not what happened.

Despite what appeared to be a relatively easy transition from life in Guatemala to life with us here in the United States, Lucy did show signs that all was not all right in her world. In the beginning she stayed very close to me, not wanting to be in another room without me. That even included when she was sleeping.

When she first came home, Lucy would fight sleep. She just didn't want to lie down or close her eyes. When she actually did sleep, out of shear exhaustion, she always awoke in a fright, immediately crying out for me to come and hold her. Even though she had slept through the night in Guatemala, once she arrived in the United States to her new home and new family, she did not soundly sleep.

I was up with her several times a night, reassuring her that she was ok, that all was well. At times she would whimper in her sleep and I would rub her back and try to soothe her. My heart ached that Lucy had fears and sadness that she was unable to verbalize. But through her actions I tried to listen to what she was trying to say.

I resisted the baby book experts who said to let the child "cry it out." But I worried that I was spoiling her by jumping to her every beck and call. There was something deep inside me that told me to follow my motherly instincts, that letting her know I was close by and holding her, loving Lucy without conditions, was what was needed in this situation at this time. The pediatrician affirmed that I was doing the right thing, giving me confidence as I trudged on, trying to get to know the little Guatemala girl, my daughter, who was struggling to change.

One month turned into two, then three, then four… I was getting used to interrupted sleep for the first time in over ten years. Dave and I had it down to a science, how to position our bodies and pillows so the little girl in the middle had sufficient space between us. We got used to the routine: Lucy crying out in the middle of the night, me rushing into her room, Lucy putting her head on my shoulder, me gently placing her on our bed, Dave moving over as far as he could to his side of the bed, Lucy curling into a little ball and falling asleep, me crawling under the covers and trying to get back to sleep…

Month four we experienced a breakthrough. Lucy slept through the night on a couple of occasions. At first I awoke, frightened. Where was Lucy? I tiptoed into her room to see her sleeping soundly in her crib. It brought me so much joy to know she was getting used to her new life and her fears were dissipating…

We are now in month five. And over the weekend I awoke for the first time to "Rock-a-bye Baby," and my heart danced! Lucy slept through the night in her crib—no disturbances or disruptions—and in the morning, at 7:30 a.m., she sat up and played with toys in her crib for the very first time!

The urge to jump to her feet, cling to the bars of her crib like a prisoner who can't wait to be freed, and cry out for help didn't happen. Lucy awoke feeling safe, secure, and happy.

Finally!

It's amazing what we take for granted. And it's amazing how time allows people to grow and change.

Now one and a half, Lucy is what we'd now call a "typical" toddler. She eats well, plays with toys, scribbles with crayons, watches *Sesame Street* and *Blue's Clues*, loves picture books and colorful balloons, and enjoys baths with lots of bubbles. Her eyes dance if she is offered an Oreo cookie or a Hershey's kiss! Fascinated with children her age, she enjoys watching them more than playing with them. Sightings of cats, dogs, squirrels, and birds make her squeal with pleasure!

And finally, when the day is done, after kissing her daddy, her sister, and her mommy goodnight, Lucy is able to rest her tired little body and her curious little mind. She is at peace with the world.

Lucinda Rubi Jean is finally "home."

Dave, Amy, Miranda, and Lucy, together forever…

Printed in the United States
41129LVS00006B/46-54